Dear Barbara,

I pray this [barcode] journal blesses you [barcode] speak to you in many ways as you journey with Him on these pages.

Love,
Sue Moliton

D0850221

Especially for

Barbara

From

Sue Molitor

Date

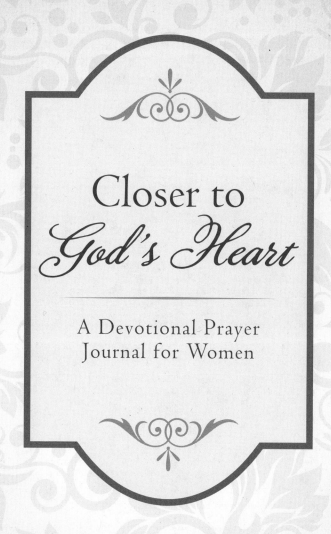

Closer to *God's Heart*

A Devotional Prayer Journal for Women

BARBOUR BOOKS

An Imprint of Barbour Publishing, Inc.

© 2015 by Barbour Publishing, Inc.

Compiled by Kathy Shutt.

Print ISBN 978-1-63058-697-3

eBookEditions:
Adobe Digital Edition(.epub) 978-1-63409-194-7
Kindle and MobiPocket Edition(.prc) 978-1-63409-195-4

All rights reserved. No part of this publication may be reproduced or transmitted for commercial purposes, except for brief quotations in printed reviews, without written permission of the publisher.

Prayers are from *180 Prayers for a Woman of God*, *Everyday Moments with God*, *Mornings with God*, and *Power Prayers to Bless Your Heart*, published by Barbour Publishing, Inc.

Churches and other noncommercial interests may reproduce portions of this book without the express written permission of Barbour Publishing, provided that the text does not exceed 500 words or 5 percent of the entire book, whichever is less, and that the text is not material quoted from another publisher. When reproducing text from this book, include the following credit line: "From *Closer to God's Heart: A Devotional Prayer Journal for Women*, published by Barbour Publishing, Inc. Used by permission."

All scripture quotations, unless otherwise noted, are taken from the King James Version of the Bible.

Scripture quotations marked NASB are taken from the New American Standard Bble, copyright © 1960, 1962, 1963, 1968, 1971, 1972, 1973, 1975, 1977, 1995 by The Lockman Foundation. Used by permission.

Scripture quotations marked NKJV are taken from the New King James Version®. Copyright © 1982 by Thomas Nelson, Inc. Used by permission. All rights reserved.

Scripture quotations marked NIV are taken from the HOLY BIBLE, NEW INTERNATIONAL VERSION®. NIV®. Copyright © 1973, 1978, 1984, 2011 by Biblica, Inc.™ Used by permission. All rights reserved worldwide.

Scripture quotations marked NLT are taken from the *Holy Bible*. New Living Translation copyright© 1996, 2004, 2007 by Tyndale House Foundation. Used by permission of Tyndale House Publishers, Inc. Carol Stream, Illinois 60188. All rights reserved.

Scripture quotations marked NCV are taken from the New Century Version of the Bible, copyright © 2005 by Thomas Nelson, Inc. Used by permission. All rights reserved.

Scripture quotations marked PHILLIPS are taken from The New Testament in Modern English, copyright © 1958, 1959, 1960 J.B. Phillips and 1947, 1952, 1955, 1957 The Macmillian Company, New York. Used by permission. All rights reserved.

Scripture quotations marked MSG are from *THE MESSAGE*. Copyright © by Eugene H. Peterson 1993, 1994, 1995, 1996, 2000, 2001, 2002. Used by permission of NavPress Publishing Group.

Published by Barbour Books, an imprint of Barbour Publishing, Inc., P.O. Box 719, Uhrichsville, Ohio 44683, www.barbourbooks.com

Our mission is to publish and distribute inspirational products offering exceptional value and biblical encouragement to the masses.

Member of the
Evangelical Christian
Publishers Association

Printed in China.

Draw Closer to God's Heart

This beautiful prayer journal is designed for those "everyday moments" in your life—the tired moments, the stressed-out moments, the joyful moments, the tearful moments, the peaceful and chaotic moments. . . Dozens of practical and encouraging prayers, complemented by related scripture selections and generous journaling space, will inspire you to strengthen your heart-connection to the heavenly Father.

As you journal your innermost thoughts and feelings alongside these prayers, may you come to know and understand that the heavenly Father really does care about *every* moment in your life!

Draw near to God and He will draw near to you.
James 4:8 NASB

The Joy of the Lord

Lord, some mornings I wake up ready to go! I feel rested and energetic. Other mornings, I wonder how I will make it through the day. Remind me that as Your child, I have a power source that is always available to me. I may not always feel joyful, but the joy of the Lord is my strength. As I spend time in Your Word, renew my strength, I pray. In Jesus' name, amen.

For the joy of the LORD is your strength.
NEHEMIAH 8:10

The One Who Is

Heavenly Father, today I'm grateful for all You are—the God who is, the God of the living, the great I Am. Your character is unchanging. You are the epitome of perfect holiness and love.

Because of who and all You are, I believe and trust in You. Your truthfulness is indisputable, and Your power is established. Not just for the majestic works by Your hand, but for the pure glory of Your nature—I worship You today. Amen.

Who is like the LORD our God, who dwells on high?
PSALM 113:5 NKJV

Use Me, Lord

Savior, You laid down Your life for me. You died a horrible death upon a cross. It was death by crucifixion, which was reserved for the worst of criminals. And You had done nothing wrong. You came into the world to save us! You gave Your very life for us. Jesus, take my life. Use me for Your kingdom's work. Only in losing my life for You will I save it. Amen.

For whosoever will save his life shall lose it; but whosoever shall lose his life for my sake and the gospel's, the same shall save it.
MARK 8:35

Power of the Word

God, I believe Your Word is true, but sometimes I have a hard time acting on it and following through with what I know is right. Help me stand on Your promises. You have put Your power behind Your Word, and I trust You to do what You have promised.

Therefore, we never stop thanking God that when you received his message from us, you didn't think of our words as mere human ideas. You accepted what we said as the very word of God—which, of course, it is. And this word continues to work in you who believe.

1 Thessalonians 2:13 nlt

Grace for Everything

Father, I'm thankful for Your *grace*—Your unmerited favor to me through Jesus Christ and that special strength You give Your children in times of need, trial, and temptation. If not for Your grace, I wouldn't even be able to approach You. Thank You for extending favor to me: forgiving my sins and adopting me into Your family. And thank You so much for that extra dose of perseverance that You keep giving to me in tough situations. I'm so thankful Your resource center will never experience a shortage. I praise You today for grace. Amen.

But he gives us more grace.
JAMES 4:6 NIV

None Like You

God, when I consider my own inadequacies, I am amazed at Your perfectness. You are truth and justice, holiness and integrity. There is none like You. You are the one and only true God. Other deities disappoint their followers; other idols fail. But You never do. Because You are perfect holiness, all Your other attributes are only good. There is no selfishness, vengefulness, or deceitfulness in You, Lord. Thus, I can trust You completely and revel in Your light unafraid. Amen.

"No one is holy like the LORD, for there is none besides You, nor is there any rock like our God."

1 SAMUEL 2:2 NKJV

Amazing Forgiveness

*L*ord, I come into Your presence thanking You for forgiveness. In a culture where many experience clinical depression because of guilt, I can know my past is redeemed because of Christ's sacrifice for me. Your forgiveness is so amazing. Although I don't deserve it, You pour it out freely and lovingly. Because You have seen fit to pardon me, I bless Your name today.

In Him we have redemption through His blood,
the forgiveness of sins, according to the riches of His grace.
EPHESIANS 1:7 NKJV

No More Sorrow

Jesus, Your disciples were dismayed. You told them You were going away but that You would see them again. Those men had walked and talked with You. You were their leader, their friend. How lost they must have felt at Your crucifixion! But three days later. . . Wow! Lord, You turn mourning into rejoicing. Help me trust in this. Thank You, Jesus. Amen.

And ye now therefore have sorrow: but I will see you again, and your heart shall rejoice, and your joy no man taketh from you.

JOHN 16:22

Putting God First

Father, a glance at my bank statement causes me to shudder. Where does my money go? Am I too concerned with what the world says I must possess to be cool, to fit in, to appear successful? Your Word says that I cannot serve both material wealth and You. I choose You, Lord. Be the master of my life and of my checkbook. I need Your help with this. Amen.

No man can serve two masters: for either he will hate the one, and love the other; or else he will hold to the one, and despise the other. Ye cannot serve God and mammon.
MATTHEW 6:24

Joyful in Hope

God, the longer I live, the more I realize that joy and hope go hand in hand. I have joy because my hope is in You. Thank You, Lord, that, as Your daughter, I do not go out to face the day in hopelessness. No matter what happens, I can find joy because my hope is not in this world or in my circumstances. My hope is in the Lord. Amen.

Happy is he that hath the God of Jacob for his help, whose hope is in the LORD his God.
PSALM 146:5

Honoring My Parents

*H*eavenly Father, show me how to honor my parents. Even as I have grown into a woman, Your command remains. Give me patience with my parents. Remind me that with age comes wisdom. Help me seek their counsel when it is appropriate. God, in Your sovereignty, You gave me the mother and father that You did. May I honor You as I honor them. Amen.

Honour thy father and thy mother, as the LORD thy God hath commanded thee.
DEUTERONOMY 5:16

My Church Family

My church is special to me in so many ways, Lord. I am so thankful that You have placed me among such a wonderful group of believers who encourage me and pray for me. Allow me to be a blessing to them, as well, and help me never forget how important they are in my life.

For our comely parts have no need: but God hath tempered the body together, having given more abundant honour to that part which lacked. That there should be no schism in the body; but that the members should have the same care one for another. And whether one member suffer, all the members suffer with it; or one member be honoured, all the members rejoice with it. Now ye are the body of Christ, and members in particular.
1 CORINTHIANS 12:24—27

Praise for God's Indescribable Gift

Thank You for giving the most precious gift, Your very own Son, so I could live each day with You. There are no words to describe the depths of Your sacrifice, but I know You did it for me. You gave Your first and only Son so You could share life with many sons and daughters. I am so thankful Jesus was willing to give His life for mine.

"For God so loved the world that he gave his one and only Son, that whoever believes in him shall not perish but have eternal life."

John 3:16 NIV

Starting Where I Am

Jesus, You give tall orders! How can I teach all nations and baptize people? Oh. . .You mean I might not even have to leave my community? There are people all around me who don't know You, Lord. Help me start with those in my sphere of influence. The grocery store clerk who seems tired and distraught. . . The teacher at my child's school who is so lost. . . Give me the courage to reach out. Amen.

Go ye therefore, and teach all nations, baptizing them in the name of the Father, and of the Son, and of the Holy Ghost.
MATTHEW 28:19

Shield of Faith

God, guard my heart and mind with the shield of faith. I will call on the name of Jesus when Satan tempts me. I will fight against his schemes to ruin me. My weapon is my knowledge of Your Word, promises memorized and cherished. My defense is my faith in Jesus Christ, my Savior. On this faith I will stand. Increase my faith and protect me from the evil one, I pray. Amen.

Above all, taking the shield of faith, wherewith ye shall be able to quench all the fiery darts of the wicked.
EPHESIANS 6:16

A Meek and Quiet Spirit

God, in Your economy a meek and quiet spirit is worth more than gold. It is not corruptible. It is eternal. Give me such a spirit. Make me a better listener, I pray. Set a guard over my tongue at times when I should not speak. Teach me to walk humbly with You, Father, and to serve people in Your name. A gracious, godly spirit is what You desire to see in me. Amen.

Whose adorning let it not be that outward adorning of plaiting the hair, and of wearing of gold, or of putting on of apparel; but let it be the hidden man of the heart, in that which is not corruptible, even the ornament of a meek and quiet spirit, which is in the sight of God of great price.

1 Peter 3:3–4

A Father

*G*od, help me remember that You're my Father. A heavenly Father—One who has unlimited resources and power, and One who has infinitely more love than any great earthly dad. When Satan tempts me to view You with suspicion, help me remember that his goal is my utter destruction. Lord, fill my heart with the truth that You love me perfectly and have only the best in mind for me. In fact, You want to embrace me, bless me, and give me heaven as my inheritance. What a wonderful Father You are! Amen.

As a father has compassion on his children, so the LORD *has compassion on those who fear him.*
PSALM 103:13 NIV

A Perfect Place

Creator God, I wish there weren't diseases in our world. Those tiny microbes that infiltrate the immune system are responsible for so much pain and grief. Although sickness was not present in the Garden of Eden—that perfect place You intended for us—it is a part of this life now, a consequence of the curse under which our world suffers. But someday You'll create a new earth, and I know bacteria won't stand a chance there. I look forward to that, Father God, for then the world will once again be "very good." Amen.

Now I saw a new heaven and a new earth, for the first heaven and
the first earth had passed away.
REVELATION 21:1 NKJV

Joy in the Name of the Lord

Father, this morning I meet You here for just a few moments before the busyness of the day takes over. I trust You. It is not always easy to trust, but You have proven trustworthy in my life. I find joy in the knowledge that You are my defender. You go before me this day into battle. I choose joy today because I love the name of the Lord Almighty. Amen.

But let all those that put their trust in thee rejoice: let them ever shout for joy, because thou defendest them: let them also that love thy name be joyful in thee.

PSALM 5:11

Joyful in Song

*H*eavenly Father, this morning I come to You with a song on my lips and joy in my heart. I thank You for all that You are doing in my life. You are at work when I sense Your presence and even when I don't. I praise You for being God. I rejoice because I am Your daughter. Amen.

---

*The L*ORD *is my strength and my shield; my heart trusted in him, and I am helped: therefore my heart greatly rejoiceth; and with my song will I praise him.*
PSALM 28:7

Take Up Your Cross

Jesus, it takes sacrifice to follow You. I have so many dreams for my life, but they are nothing unless they include You. Help me let go of the things I selfishly desire and that aren't meant to be a part of my life. Your purposes for my life mean success. I give You my life—I completely surrender.

Then he said to the crowd, "If any of you wants to be my follower, you must turn from your selfish ways, take up your cross daily, and follow me."

LUKE 9:23 NLT

Asking for God's Help

Sometimes I feel You have so much on Your plate that I should work things out on my own. I know I shouldn't feel like I'm bothering You, but my problems seem small compared to what others deal with. Still, I know You want to help me. You are just waiting for me to ask, so I'm asking—please, help. You know what I'm dealing with. Forgive me for not coming to You sooner. I accept Your help today.

God is my helper; the Lord is with those who uphold my life.
PSALM 54:4 NKJV

Serve One Another

God, I have not been put on this earth to serve myself. It is not all about me. Sometimes I forget that! Service is what this life is all about, isn't it? Father, give me opportunities to show love to others today. Make every moment a "God moment." Help me be aware of the many needs around me. Create in me a heart that loves others and puts them ahead of myself. Amen.

For, brethren, ye have been called unto liberty; only use not liberty for an occasion to the flesh, but by love serve one another. For all the law is fulfilled in one word, even in this; Thou shalt love thy neighbour as thyself.

GALATIANS 5:13—14

Opportunities to Serve

*F*ather, with this new day, give me new eyes. Show me the hungry, the lonely, the tired. Show me those who need encouragement, those who need a friend, those who need to see Jesus in me. I don't want to miss the chances that You give me to be a blessing to others. I know that when I serve others, the heart of my Creator is blessed. Make me aware of others' needs, I ask. Amen.

And the King shall answer and say unto them, Verily I say unto you, Inasmuch as ye have done it unto one of the least of these my brethren, ye have done it unto me.
MATTHEW 25:40

....

....

....

....

....

....

....

....

....

....

....

....

Knowing God's Mercy

*F*ather, You love me with no strings attached. No matter what I do or don't do, You show me grace that makes me love You more. Everywhere I turn, Your eyes are on me, caring for me with a compassion greater than the love I could ever experience from anyone else. Thank You for Your promise that Your mercy follows me all the days of my life.

For the LORD your God is a merciful God; he will not abandon or destroy you or forget the covenant with your forefathers, which he confirmed to them by oath.

DEUTERONOMY 4:31 NIV

Reflecting God's Love to Others

Lord, I truly want to influence my little corner of the world for Christ. Sometimes I can relate to the persecution that the heroes of the Bible experienced. It stings when someone sarcastically says, "Pray for me!" Help me remember that I should never be ashamed of my faith. Give me a kind spirit and a gentleness that reflects Your love, regardless of the circumstances. Amen.

Having a good conscience; that, whereas they speak evil of you, as of evildoers, they may be ashamed that falsely accuse your good conversation in Christ.
1 Peter 3:16

A Giving Heart

Father, may I be honest? Sometimes I don't feel like serving. They keep asking if I will help with this or that at church. And there is always a collection being taken up. Can't I just focus on me? I have my own needs! But oh, the peace I feel when I lay my head on my pillow at night knowing I have loved with action, with sacrifice. Make me a giver, I ask. Amen.

Remember the words of the Lord Jesus, how he said,
It is more blessed to give than to receive.
ACTS 20:35

....

....

....

....

....

....

....

....

....

....

....

....

....

Cheerfulness

Jesus, I can't imagine You as a sour, solemn man. I believe You enjoyed life immensely, and I know You brought joy to those around You. Why else would "sinners and tax collectors" want to eat with You (as Your enemies pointed out)? Your mission on this planet was sacred and grave; but I believe Your demeanor in everyday life was buoyant and pleasant. Others loved being in Your presence. Help me pattern my daily attitude after Your example and take heed of Your command to "be of good cheer." Let me reflect You by the way I approach living. Amen.

"Be of good cheer, daughter."
MATTHEW 9:22 NKJV

Avoiding Idleness

Lord, I know that You want me to take care of my household. Sometimes I am so tempted to put off my duties around the house, and I find myself spending too much time on the computer or the telephone. Help me be balanced. Help me take care of my household and be aware of the trap of idleness. I know that procrastination is not a good or godly habit. Amen.

She looketh well to the ways of her household, and eateth not the bread of idleness.
PROVERBS 31:27

A God-Centered Home

*F*ather, so many homes are shaken up these days. So many families are shattering to pieces around me. Protect my home, I pray. Protect my loved ones. Be the foundation of my home, strong and solid, consistent and wise. May every decision made here reflect Your principles. May those who visit this home and encounter this family be keenly aware of our uniqueness because we serve the one true and almighty God. Amen.

Except the LORD build the house, they labour in vain that build it: except the LORD keep the city, the watchman waketh but in vain.

PSALM 127:1

A Godly Example

God, help me be an example of a faithful disciple of Christ to my family and friends. Those who are close in our lives have the ability to lead us toward or away from righteousness and godliness. I pray that all I do and say will honor You and that I will never be a stumbling block to others. May all within my sphere of influence find me faithful to You. Amen.

The righteous is more excellent than his neighbour: but the way of the wicked seduceth them.
PROVERBS 12:26

....

....

....

....

....

....

....

....

....

....

....

....

....

....

....

Resisting the Urge to Gossip

*F*ather, men don't seem to struggle with gossip the way we ladies do. A juicy tidbit of information is so tempting! I need Your help, Lord, to resist the temptation to gossip. Your Word warns me of the dangers of gossip and slander. Strengthen me so that I will not be a troublemaker but rather, a peacemaker. Help me resist the urge to listen to or speak gossip. Amen.

A froward man soweth strife: and a whisperer separateth chief friends.
PROVERBS 16:28

Trust in the Lord

*F*ather, I lean on my own understanding, don't I? Help me trust that You know what is best. Often I make plans and attempt to figure things out when I should submit it all to You in prayer. Bring to mind, as I sit quietly before You now, the times in the past when You have come through for me. Give me faith for my future, knowing that it is in my Father's hands. Amen.

Trust in the LORD with all thine heart; and lean not unto thine own understanding.
In all thy ways acknowledge him, and he shall direct thy paths.
PROVERBS 3:5–6

Increase My Faith

Lord, my faith is small. Thank You for the promise in Your Word that You can work with even a mustard seed of faith! I submit my lack of faith to You and ask that You grow and stretch my trust in You. I want my faith to be great. As I meditate on Your love for me, please increase my faith that You are sovereign and You will take care of all my needs. Amen.

Verily I say unto you, If ye have faith as a grain of mustard seed, ye shall say unto this mountain, Remove hence to yonder place; and it shall remove; and nothing shall be impossible unto you.

MATTHEW 17:20

Faith Pleases God

Father, I read of Enoch, Noah, Abraham, and Joseph. I know the stories of Sarah and Rahab. The Bible is full of men and women of faith. Those who pleased You were not those who were the wealthiest, most beautiful, or had the most important names. What pleases You, my Father, is faith. Without it, I cannot please You. I choose to live by faith as my spiritual ancestors lived. Strengthen my faith, I ask. Amen.

But without faith it is impossible to please him: for he that cometh to God must believe that he is, and that he is a rewarder of them that diligently seek him.

HEBREWS 11:6

Just Do It

Dear Lord, I want to have an obedient heart. Sometimes when You speak to me, I feel hesitation or want to postpone what You're telling me to do. Yet that means either I don't trust You or I want my own way, neither of which is good. A child ought to obey her parents because she acknowledges their right to direct her and because she trusts the love behind their words. Help me, Lord, to embrace that kind of attitude when You speak to me. In Christ's name, amen.

But be doers of the word, and not hearers only, deceiving yourselves.
JAMES 1:22 NKJV

True Joy

Thank You, Father, for Your Word, which teaches me how to experience true joy. This world sends me a lot of messages through the media and through those who do not know You. I have tried some of the things that are supposed to bring joy, but they always leave me empty in the end. Thank You for the truth. Help me abide in You, that I might be overflowing with joy. Amen.

These things have I spoken unto you, that my joy might remain in you,
and that your joy might be full.
JOHN 15:11

Joy in God's Word

Thank You, God, that in Your holy scriptures I find the ways of life. I find wise counsel on the pages of my Bible. You reveal the truth to me, Lord, and there is no greater blessing than to know the truth. You tell me in Your Word that the truth sets me free. I am free to live a life that brings You glory and honor. May others see the joy I have found in You! Amen.

Thou hast made known to me the ways of life; thou shalt make me full of joy with thy countenance.
ACTS 2:28

Glorifying God in My Work

God, today as I work both in my home and outside of it, may my attitude glorify You. I am not of this world, but I am in it, and often it has too much influence on me. May I think twice before I grumble, Father, about the tasks set before me this day. I will choose to work as unto my Father, and may my countenance reflect Your love to those around me. Amen.

And whatsoever ye do, do it heartily, as to the Lord, and not unto men; Knowing that of the Lord ye shall receive the reward of the inheritance: for ye serve the Lord Christ.
COLOSSIANS 3:23–24

What Would Jesus Do?

Heavenly Father, sometimes I am a Sunday Christian. How I want to worship You with the rest of my week! Please help me be mindful of You throughout the week. May Your will and Your ways permeate my thoughts and decisions. Whether I am taking care of things at home or working with others in the workplace, may I glorify You in all that I say and do. Amen.

Whether therefore ye eat, or drink, or whatsoever ye do, do all to the glory of God.
1 CORINTHIANS 10:31

The Power of God's Protection

*F*airy tales and fables always have a hero—a rescuer, protector, and conqueror. God, You created me and gave me life. You are the One who saves my life every day. You have given Your angels charge over me to keep me protected. You go before me and fight my battles, sometimes without me ever knowing those battles exist. You are my refuge and my shield. Thank You for always being there.

For the LORD your God is He who goes with you, to fight for you
against your enemies, to save you.
DEUTERONOMY 20:4 NKJV

....
....
....
....
....
....
....
....
....
....
....
....

Every Good Gift

Father, thank You for the blessings You have poured out on my family. Often I dwell on that which we do not have. Please remind me to be ever grateful for so many gifts. The comforts we enjoy each day, like running water and electricity, are so easily taken for granted. Thank You for Your provision in our lives. Help me have a thankful heart so that my family might be more thankful also. Amen.

And thou shalt rejoice in every good thing which the LORD thy God hath given unto thee, and unto thine house, thou, and the Levite, and the stranger that is among you.

DEUTERONOMY 26:11

Iron Sharpens Iron

Lord, I find it hard to talk to my friends about areas of their lives in which they are not honoring You. And I certainly do not always appreciate their correction in my life! Father, allow such sweet, godly fellowship between my Christian sisters and me that when truth should be spoken in love, we are able to speak into one another's lives. We need one another. Iron sharpens iron. Amen.

Iron sharpeneth iron; so a man sharpeneth the countenance of his friend.
PROVERBS 27:17

A Beautiful Work

Lord, I read of the woman who poured out a flask of expensive perfume upon Your feet. The disciples did not understand, but You saw it as a beautiful work. Give me a heart like hers. Whatever I possess, whatever comes my way, help me fling it all forth for Your glory. Let me use it wisely but extravagantly to honor my King. I love You, Lord. Make my life a beautiful work for You. Amen.

But when his disciples saw it, they had indignation, saying, To what purpose is this waste?
For this ointment might have been sold for much, and given to the poor.
When Jesus understood it, he said unto them, Why trouble ye the woman?
for she hath wrought a good work upon me.
MATTHEW 26:8–10

Joyful Regardless of Circumstances

Lord, there are days when I can't help but rejoice in what You are doing. But many times the daily grind is just rather humdrum. There is nothing to rejoice about, much less give thanks for! Or is there? Help me, Father, be joyful and thankful every day. Each day is a gift from You. Remind me of this truth today, and give me a joyful, thankful heart, I ask. Amen.

Rejoice evermore. Pray without ceasing. In every thing give thanks: for this is the will of God in Christ Jesus concerning you.
1 Thessalonians 5:16–18

A Witness in My Community

Lord, there are so many people in my community who either don't care about You or who think they will please You by their own merit; but several of them don't truly know You. I ask You to open doors so I may witness to them. My prayer is that many will come to You.

But whoso hath this world's good, and seeth his brother have need, and shutteth up his bowels of compassion from him, how dwelleth the love of God in him?

1 John 3:17

The Gift of Salvation

Dear Father, thank You for the gift of salvation, for sending Your only Son to be a sacrifice for all people, even those who didn't want Him. I am in awe of Your mercy extended to me. It is incredible to think that I am a daughter of God. Thank You, Jesus: You didn't walk away from the cross, but You laid down Your life for me. Thank You, Holy Spirit, for drawing me to this greatest of gifts. My life is forever changed. In Christ's name, amen.

For the grace of God has appeared that offers salvation to all people.
TITUS 2:11 NIV

Filled with Contentment

Sometimes my attitude is so "poor me" that I even get sick, Father. I keep thinking that if only I could have this or that, life would be easier. I know I'm missing out on a truly abundant life by whining so much, and I ask You to forgive me. Fill me with contentment. Amen.

Not that I speak in respect of want: for I have learned,
in whatsoever state I am, therewith to be content.
PHILIPPIANS 4:11

Internal Clocks

*H*eavenly Father, it appears as though every person has an internal rhythm seemingly permanently set to a certain time of the day. There are early birds and night owls and middle-of-the-day people. Not many of us are successful in changing our internal clock, Lord. Maybe You wanted to create humans with varying peak hours of energy. It would be a pretty boring world if we all fizzled out at the same time each day. Thank You for the variety You have provided in all of us. Amen.

To declare Your lovingkindness in the morning, and Your faithfulness every night.
Psalm 92:2 nkjv

Never Give Up

*L*ord, I don't want to be a quitter, but I've tried so hard to be like You, and I keep messing up. I know You said that with You all things are possible, and I need to be reminded of that daily. Don't let me give up. Help me remember that You aren't finished with me yet. Amen.

Wherefore, my beloved, as ye have always obeyed, not as in my presence only, but now much more in my absence, work out your own salvation with fear and trembling. For it is God which worketh in you both to will and to do of his good pleasure.

PHILIPPIANS 2:12–13

Influenced by Scripture

God, Your Word is such a gift. Often I get so busy that I neglect my reading of it. As I open Your Word this morning, use scripture to influence my actions and reactions throughout this day. As I reflect on where I invest most of my time, help me choose a time and place to read Your Word each day. What could be more important? Thank You for Your holy Word. Amen.

And that from a child thou hast known the holy scriptures, which are able to make thee wise unto salvation through faith which is in Christ Jesus. All scripture is given by inspiration of God, and is profitable for doctrine, for reproof, for correction, for instruction in righteousness.
2 Timothy 3:15–16

Provisions from God

God, there is no creature on earth You do not see or provide for. I'm bringing praise to You right now for the daily things You supply for me. It is through Your goodness that I have food to eat, clothes to wear, and water to drink. Help me always be thankful for what I have and to not emulate the wandering Israelites, who, focusing on lack, preferred to complain. Your power is awesome; thank You for generously supplying my needs and wants each and every day.

You open Your hand and satisfy the desire of every living thing.
PSALM 145:16 NKJV

The Inspirational Word

Lord, Your Word thrills me, convicts me, comforts me, and strengthens me. I am so thankful that You gave us the Bible. Thank You for inspiring the prophets of old as they penned Your truth. Thank You for protecting the scripture through centuries of skepticism and persecution. Thank You for giving me the blessing of this treasure, for allowing me to hold it in my hand. When I am hungry, Your Word feeds me; when I am fearful, it assures me; when I am uncertain, it guides me. Your Book is the light upon my path. Without it, I would be lost. Amen.

All Scripture is God-breathed and is useful for teaching, rebuking,
coreecting and training in righteousness.
2 TIMOTHY 3:16 NIV

Diverse Gifts

*D*ear God, today the fellowship of other believers ministered to me. There are times when I get frustrated with the church—it has its challenges. But so does a human body. And yet when each bodily organ serves the function for which it was made, there is life, energy, and passion. Help me remember, Lord, that You made my spiritual brothers and sisters with diverse gifts; help me work with them, not against them. Thank You for reminding me again today that this family of God is one of Your treasures, a blessing from Your hand—and heart. Amen.

There are different kinds of gifts, but the same Spirit distributes them.
1 Corinthians 12:4 niv

To Every Generation

*J*ehovah God, I come just now to revel in Your faithfulness. From generations past to this very minute, multitudes have testified that You always come through. Yet there have been times in my life when I thought You had overlooked me, that You weren't aware of my needs, that You didn't hear my prayers. But my doubts proved false, and Your record is untarnished. You didn't promise that I would always understand Your ways, but You did promise Your presence and love in every circumstance. And I can testify it's true. I love You, Lord. Amen.

Your faithfulness endures to all generations.
PSALM 119:90 NKJV

The Past Is Gone

Father, I'm glad You have redeemed my past. I've said and done things of which I'm not proud. I'm grateful that You've blotted out my sins and given me a fresh start. Like one using a marker board, You wiped away the shame and guilt and handed the marker back to me. I don't have to live in the past; I can face the future with confidence and grace. In Christ's name, amen.

As far as the east is from the west, so far has He removed our transgressions from us.

PSALM 103:12 NKJV

The Power of God's Closeness

God, I am depending on my own abilities. I don't want to feel far from You, but I do. Yet being close to You is more than a feeling. As I draw closer to You, I know You will draw closer to me. Your presence gives me an inner strength that is not my own. Let me experience You as if You were standing close enough that I could feel Your breath on my face.

What other great nation has gods that are intimate with them the way GOD, our God, is with us, always ready to listen to us?
DEUTERONOMY 4:7 MSG

Thanks for My Friends

Thank You, Lord, for my friends. I appreciate that they accept me for who I am and encourage me to grow in my relationship with You. They want to see me succeed in every area of my life. They are there for me when I need them, concerned for my life just as I am for theirs. Thank You for the courage to be open and truthful with them. You have joined our hearts together with Your love.

The soul of Jonathan was knit to the soul of David,
and Jonathan loved him as his own soul.
1 Samuel 18:1 nkjv

Choosing Friends Wisely

*Y*our Word says two are better than one, because if one falls, there will be someone to lift that person up. Lord, I ask for divine connections, good friends only You can give. Help me let go of relationships that are unhealthy and negative. I want friends who speak and live positively, who inspire and encourage but also tell me the truth when I need to hear it. Give me wisdom today in the relationships I choose.

The godly give good advice to their friends; the wicked lead them astray.
PROVERBS 12:26 NLT

To Look to the Heart

*Y*ou know the hearts of everyone, Lord. At first glance, all I see is outward appearances. I want to be a good judge of character. Help me be discerning. Make me aware when I am being negatively influenced or manipulated. Teach me what I need to know to be a quality friend, and show me the hearts of my friends.

As for those who seemed to be important—whatever they were makes no difference to me;
God does not judge by external appearance.
GALATIANS 2:6 NIV

In the Face of Prejudice

All men and women are equal in Your sight. Jesus died for every one of us, no matter where we come from or what color our skin is. Help me avoid valuing one relationship over another because of influence, wealth, intellect, or race. Help me see others from Your perspective, no matter how different other people are from me. Help me love them and learn from the differences we have.

Therefore, accept each other just as Christ has accepted you so that God will be given glory.
ROMANS 15:7 NLT

Complete Surrender

Lord, I'm scared. I am scheduled for medical tests soon. I know my body is temporal and made of dust, but I truly don't want there to be something wrong with it physically. Yet help me surrender to what You have decided for me. Still, I'm earthly. . .and seen from my perspective, the situation is really frightening. Show me how to trust You minute by minute—not in the hope that everything will be as I want, but in the certainty that You've thought of every angle of my life and You are in control of all the details. Amen.

When I am afraid, I put my trust in you.
PSALM 56:3 NIV

Showing Mercy

Jesus, like the Good Samaritan in Your parable, may I show mercy. Some may never enter the doors of a church, but what a difference an act of grace could make! Put before me opportunities glorifying god to show unmerited favor. That is, after all, what You have shown to me. You died for my sins. I could never have earned salvation. It is a free gift, an act of grace. Make me merciful. Amen.

Which now of these three, thinkest thou, was neighbour unto him that fell among the thieves? And he said, He that shewed mercy on him. Then said Jesus unto him, Go, and do thou likewise.
LUKE 10:36—37

Father, I tend to seek the glory for myself. It is human nature, I know, but I want to be different. I am Your daughter. Let me shine, and when others ask me, "Why the smile?" or "Why the good deeds?" let me point them to You. You are the source of all that is good in me. You have given me each ability I have. May I reflect Your love through my good works. Amen.

Let your light so shine before men, that they may see your good works,
and glorify your Father which is in heaven.
Matthew 5:16

A Choice to Serve God

*F*ather, it is a daily choice. Will I serve the world? Myself? Or my God? What will I model for the children in my life who look up to me? Will my family and friends know me as one who is self-serving or kingdom-focused? Today I make the choice to serve the Lord. Help me truly live as Your servant in this world. Amen.

As for me and my house, we will serve the LORD.
JOSHUA 24:15

The Value of Fellowship

Heavenly Father, I pray that You will not allow me to isolate myself. I need fellowship with other believers. I benefit from spending time with my Christian friends. You tell us in Your Word that it is not good to be alone. We need one another as we walk through this life with all of its ups and downs. When I am tempted to distance myself from others, guide me back into Christian fellowship. Amen.

Two are better than one; because they have a good reward for their labour. For if they fall, the one will lift up his fellow: but woe to him that is alone when he falleth; for he hath not another to help him up.
ECCLESIASTES 4:9–10

Pure Motives

*L*ord, help me examine my motives in pursuit of friendship. Why do I seek relationships with certain people? Give me the courage to look truthfully into my heart and see my true intentions. Sometimes I think a relationship with a certain person might help me look better in the eyes of others. I am ambitious, but I know it's wrong to use people to get what I want. You supply everything I need. Help me maintain right and pure relationships before You.

To flatter friends is to lay a trap for their feet.
PROVERBS 29:5 NLT

God Is Faithful

God, I focus a lot on my faith in You. And then You show me that it is not all about me. You are faithful to me. You show me how to be faithful. You never leave. You never give up on me. You never turn away. You always show up. You always believe in me. You are faithful by your very nature. You cannot be unfaithful. Thank You for Your faithfulness in my life. Amen.

But the Lord is faithful, who shall stablish you, and keep you from evil.
2 Thessalonians 3:3

Saved by Grace through Faith

God, it is so comforting to know that my position before You is secure. Thank You for seeing me through a new lens. When You look at me, because I have been saved through faith, You see Your Son in me. You no longer see sin but righteousness. I couldn't have earned it, no matter how hard I worked. Thank You for the gift of salvation through my faith in Jesus. Amen.

For by grace are ye saved through faith; and that not of yourselves:
it is the gift of God: Not of works, lest any man should boast.
EPHESIANS 2:8–9

....

....

....

....

....

....

....

....

....

....

....

....

What Is My "Isaac"?

*H*eavenly Father, I am amazed by the faith of Abraham. He offered up his son, Isaac, the one for whom he had waited and waited, the promised one. When You tested his faith, he answered immediately. He rose up early in the morning and acted on Your command. Would I have had the faith that Abraham had in You? Would I trust You even in my worst nightmare? I hope so. How I hope so. Amen.

By faith Abraham, when he was tried, offered up Isaac: and he that had received the promises offered up his only begotten son, Of whom it was said, That in Isaac shall thy seed be called: Accounting that God was able to raise him up, even from the dead; from whence also he received him in a figure.

HEBREWS 11:17–19

Praying for Bold Faith

I desire a bold faith, Jesus. Like the woman who followed You, crying out, asking that You cast a demon from her daughter. She was a Gentile, not a Jew; yet, she called You the "Son of David." She acknowledged You as the Messiah. And You stopped. Her faith impressed You. You healed the child. May I be so bold. May I recognize that You are the only solution to every problem. Amen.

Then Jesus answered and said unto her, O woman, great is thy faith: be it unto thee even as thou wilt. And her daughter was made whole from that very hour.
MATTHEW 15:28

Trying of My Faith

Father, Your Word tells me that You have begun a good work in me, and You will be faithful to complete it. Help me resist the temptation to sin. I know that it's a process and that no one is perfect, but I desire to grow in my faith. I want to be a faithful daughter of the King. Bless my efforts, Father, and strengthen me as only You can. Amen.

My brethren, count it all joy when ye fall into divers temptations; Knowing this, that the trying of your faith worketh patience. But let patience have her perfect work, that ye may be perfect and entire, wanting nothing.

JAMES 1:2−4

Walking by Faith

God, one day my faith shall be sight. In this life, I am called to walk by faith. In the next, I will see that which I have believed in for all these years. Earth is for faith, and heaven is for sight. Continue to nurture in me a deep faith, one that causes me to take each step of this journey with You as my focus. I walk by faith, not by sight. Amen.

For we walk by faith, not by sight.
2 Corinthians 5:7

Patience in a Busy World

*F*ather, patience isn't easy. This is a busy, fast-paced world in which I exist! I drive through fast-food restaurant windows and receive hot food within a few minutes. Automated bank tellers provide cash in an instant. There is not much I have to wait for in this modern age. But I realize that some of the things that matter most require great patience. Teach me to wait with grace. Amen.

Now we exhort you, brethren, warn them that are unruly, comfort the feebleminded, support the weak, be patient toward all men.

1 THESSALONIANS 5:14

Waiting for Christ's Return

*L*ord Jesus, the evening news reports are full of sadness. At times I wonder why You are waiting. Why don't You come back for Your people? Why don't You take us out of this world full of sin and pain? I know there is a better place, another life waiting for us in heaven. Give me patience. No one knows the day that You will return. As I wait, may I keep my eyes fixed on You. Amen.

Be patient therefore, brethren, unto the coming of the Lord. Behold, the husbandman waiteth for the precious fruit of the earth, and hath long patience for it, until he receive the early and latter rain. Be ye also patient; stablish your hearts: for the coming of the Lord draweth nigh.

JAMES 5:7–8

Patient but Not Lazy

*J*esus, there is so much work to be done. There are so many who have not heard the Good News of Christ yet! As Your people, we must be about kingdom work and spreading the Gospel. You have given us the great commission to go into the world and tell others. But we must also be patient in our faith as we await the perfect timing of Your second coming! Amen.

That ye be not slothful, but followers of them who through faith and patience inherit the promises.
HEBREWS 6:12

Patience with Others

Father, make me a little bit more like Jesus each day. Make me sensitive to the Holy Spirit when I am tempted to be impatient. Let me be known as one who is kind, merciful, and humble. When others describe me, I am not sure they would use these adjectives. Just as You bear with me, help me bear with my family, friends, and colleagues with a spirit of forgiveness. Amen.

Put on therefore, as the elect of God, holy and beloved, bowels of mercies, kindness, humbleness of mind, meekness, longsuffering; Forbearing one another, and forgiving one another, if any man have a quarrel against any: even as Christ forgave you, so also do ye.
COLOSSIANS 3:12—13

Slow to Anger

Lord, like a virus, a spirit of dissatisfaction spreads quickly. It can infect everyone who comes near. You warn me in Your Word about this. You want Your people to be slow to anger. Help me be aware of the impact my attitude and my reactions have on those within my sphere of influence. I truly want to be a peacemaker and not one who is known for stirring up trouble. Amen.

A wrathful man stirreth up strife: but he that is slow to anger appeaseth strife.
PROVERBS 15:18

Following Christ's Example

*L*ord, You are always there, and You are consistently patient with me. What if it were not so? What if You reached Your limit and showed the wrath that I deserve in my sinful imperfection? Because of Your great patience with me, let me not grow tired of being patient myself. Let me model what You have shown me by Your example. Thank You for Your great patience with me, God. Amen.

And let us not be weary in well doing: for in due season we shall reap, if we faint not.
GALATIANS 6:9

....

....

....

....

....

....

....

....

....

....

....

....

....

....

Renewing My Strength

*H*eavenly Father, I am amazed by all the energy drinks and power bars available these days at the grocery store. If only everyone could see that true strength, true energy comes from You! Certainly exercise and good nutrition are helpful. But inner strength, the type that endures life's hardships and trials, is found only in a relationship with Christ. I am so thankful I have this great source of strength. Amen.

But they that wait upon the L*ORD* *shall renew their strength; they shall mount up with wings as eagles; they shall run, and not be weary; and they shall walk, and not faint.*
ISAIAH 40:31

Patience and Wisdom

*F*ather, patience and wisdom seem to go hand in hand. I am beginning to determine that the wisest people I know are also some of the most patient. They seek You in every trial. They exhibit Your character traits. Give me patience. Help me be still before You and seek You in my life. May I grow in wisdom through being patient as You teach and stretch me. Amen.

But the wisdom that is from above is first pure, then peaceable, gentle, and easy to be intreated, full of mercy and good fruits, without partiality, and without hypocrisy.
JAMES 3:17

....

....

....

....

....

....

....

....

....

....

....

....

....

....

Blessed Are the Flexible

Flexibility is a struggle for me, God. I don't like interruptions in my routine. It's challenging for me to accept a rerouting of my day. Still, sometimes You have to reorganize for me, because I haven't recognized Your promptings. Or maybe there's someone You need me to meet or a disaster You want me to avoid. Help me accept the detours in my plan today, aware of Your sovereignty over all. Amen.

This is the day the LORD has made; we will rejoice and be glad in it.
PSALM 118:24 NKJV

For Stability in Relationships

*L*ord, I ask for You to stabilize my family relationships. Help us overcome the things that cause us to push each other away. Teach us to be steady and strong for one another. Show us how we can honor each other. Soften our hearts and help us forgive if we feel we've been wronged.

He is like a man building a house, who dug down deep and laid the foundation on rock. When a flood came, the torrent struck that house but could not shake it, because it was well built.
LUKE 6:48 NIV

For All Eternity

Lord, help me recognize that eternity is now. We are eternal beings, and the things we do today are the beginning of forever. I want to spend eternity with my family members. Remind us that each day is a gift and that our time is precious. Help us not waste it with idle words and quarrelling. Thank You for giving us Your wisdom to make the most of every moment; to build each other up in faith.

Better is a dish of vegetables where love is than a fattened ox served with hatred.
PROVERBS 15:17 NASB

Slice of Life

*D*ear Lord, the transition of minutes to hours is so incremental that it is tedious to observe. It's much easier to focus on large chunks of time than a myriad of tiny ones. Yet hours are made up of minutes, just like the body is comprised of cells. Each is vital to the whole. Lord, help me remember that each minute of the day is a small section, a slice of my life. Help me make the best use of every minute. Amen.

Make the best use of your time, despite all the difficulties of these days.
Ephesians 5:16 Phillips

Strength to Stand

Lord, as large as my family is, there are bound to be some members whose life views are significantly different than mine. At times this gets annoying, particularly when they attempt to force their outlook on me. Give me the strength to stand for what I know to be true, and help me love my family despite our differences.

In the day when I cried thou answeredst me,
and strengthenedst me with strength in my soul.
PSALM 138:3

....

....

....

....

....

....

....

....

....

....

....

....

....

....

Getting Started

Dear Lord, the first step toward any goal is the hardest, and I just don't feel motivated to take it. But there are things I need to do, and so far I haven't found a fairy to do them for me. Procrastination is a terrible hindrance. I know. I'm a closet procrastinator. I don't like to admit to it, but You see it anyway. Thank You for giving me more chances than I deserve. Remind me that I just need to start. Inspiration often springs from soil watered with obedience. Let me learn this lesson well. Amen.

The way of the sluggard is blocked with thorns.
PROVERBS 15:19 NIV

_____

_____

_____

_____

_____

_____

_____

_____

_____

_____

_____

_____

_____

Difficult People

Dear Lord, I ask You to help me be patient and kind today. The Bible speaks about long-suffering. That's what I need as I deal with difficult people and irritating situations. Whether it's squabbling children or rude drivers or harried clerks, I know there will be those today who will irk me. In those moments when I want to scream, help me remember to forbear and forgive. It's just so easy to react, but help me instead deliberately choose my response. I'm depending on Your power, Father. Amen.

Bear with each other and forgive one another if any of you
has a grievance against someone.
COLOSSIANS 3:13 NIV

Wise Fear

"The fear of the Lord is the beginning of wisdom" (Psalm 111:10). Sometimes this passage from Your Word seems almost contradictory, Lord. But there is healthy fear, and then there's rippling fear. I know this passage means that my respect for You is so deep that I abhor sin. Please help me have this wise fear. Amen.

*The fear of the LORD is the beginning of wisdom: and the knowledge
of the holy is understanding.*
PROVERBS 9:10

....

....

....

....

....

....

....

....

....

....

....

....

....

....

Unlimited Resources

*F*ather, the Bible says You own "the cattle on a thousand hills." You have unlimited resources. So I'm asking You to supply a special need I have today. Although I try to be a good steward of the money You give me, some unexpected event has caught me without the necessary funds. I know You can remedy this situation, if You deem that good for me. Because You're my Father, I'm asking for Your financial advice. I need Your wisdom in this area of my life. Amen.

"For every animal of the forest is mine, and the cattle on a thousand hills."
PSALM 50:10 NIV

Lost!

Lord, I've lost my cell phone again! Please help me find it! I know sometimes I'm careless; help me learn from this. But, Lord, You know how much information is in that phone and how much I need it to carry out my responsibilities today. You know where it is right now. Help me think of that place. Guide me to it. And just like the woman with the lost coin—I will rejoice! Amen.

"Rejoice with me, for I have found the piece which I lost!"
Luke 15:9 nkjv

A Proper Outlook

So often, Lord, I see relationships crumbling, and much of the time a money issue is what starts the process. Some people are careless or dishonest in their spending; others just want too much. As a result there is a lot of bitterness and hatred. Please help me have a proper outlook when money is involved.

He that loveth silver shall not be satisfied with silver; nor he that loveth abundance with increase: this is also vanity.
ECCLESIASTES 5:10

God Is a Shield

Protector God, today I'm remembering someone in the armed forces. Though I know war wasn't in Your original plan for this world, it has become a necessary tool for overcoming evil. The Bible recounts stories of You leading Your people, the Israelites, into battle to defend what was right. So there is honor in defending freedom and justice. I ask You to protect this one from danger; dispatch Your peace, and put a hedge before, behind, and around him. Watch over all those who are putting their lives in harm's way for my sake. In Christ's name, amen.

He shields all who take refuge in him. . . . He trains my hands for battle; my arms can bend a bow of bronze. You make your saving help my shield.
PSALM 18:30, 34–35 NIV

A Shining Light

*D*ear God, I want to be a better witness for You. I have friends and family members who don't know You, and every day I interact with people who aren't believers. Lord, I don't want to be corny or pushy, but I do want to let my light shine before others. I ask You to open up the doors for me today. Let me sense Your prompting. And let the silent witness of my life also speak to others about Your great plan of salvation. In Jesus' name, amen.

Preach the word; be instant in season, out of season;
reprove, rebuke, exhort with all long suffering and doctrine.
2 TIMOTHY 4:2

Extras

*D*ear God, I am so thankful that You have provided for me. Sometimes that blessing even goes above and beyond my needs. I now ask for wisdom in handling these gifts. My desire is to glorify You and to make sure that I'm not controlled by money. Please help me use it in a way that honors You. Amen.

But my God shall supply all your need according to his riches in glory by Christ Jesus.
PHILIPPIANS 4:19

....

....

....

....

....

....

....

....

....

....

....

....

....

....

Keep Me

Dear Father, in the scurry of life, I often forget to be thankful for important things. So many times You've shielded my family from physical harm, and I didn't know it until later. And I'm sure I don't even know about all those moments when You've guarded us from spiritual danger. Although we are the apple of Your eye, I realize we're not immune to trauma and disaster; You won't remove the effects of the curse until the right time comes. But for now, I'm grateful that You care about us and that the only way something can touch us is after it's passed Your gentle inspection. Amen.

Keep me as the apple of the eye, hide me under the shadow of thy wings.
PSALM 17:8

Employer Woes

*G*od, I have the most demanding boss ever. I need to demonstrate the love of Christ, but it can be challenging when my superior is, at times, so hard to please. Give me courage, Lord, to rise above my emotions. Help me pray for my boss as the Bible tells me to and serve as though it is an assignment from You. For You, Lord, are my true superior. Bless my boss today, God, and show Your love to him through me. Amen.

Whatever you do, work at it with all your heart, as working for the Lord, not for human masters.
COLOSSIANS 3:23–24 NIV

Trusting God for Safety

*F*ather, I follow hard after You. I will not be distracted and will choose to be at the right place at the right time, every time. Thank You for keeping me safe today. I am secure because You have made Your angels responsible for protecting me at all times. Disasters are far from me because I walk on the path of safety.

In righteousness you will be established: Tyranny will be far from you; you will have nothing to fear. Terror will be far removed; it will not come near you.

ISAIAH 54:14 NIV

Trusting God for My Future

My life is an obstacle course filled with things that try to keep me off balance. But I draw strength from You. When I pray, I know You hear me. You make plans for me to have a successful life and a prosperous future. I cannot fail because You are directing me as I look to You for guidance. Thank You, Lord, that no matter how many times I fall, You always reach down to take my hand and help me up again.

If God is for us, who can be against us?
ROMANS 8:31 NIV

Sibling Revelry

*H*eavenly Father, thank You for my siblings. When the chips are really down, I can depend on them. They know my background, my temperament, and my journey. We share the same blood and the same basic life philosophy. When we were kids, we squabbled a lot, but now, I just love getting a call from one of them. They understand me like no one else. And I pray we'll always be there for one another. Bless my brothers and sisters today. In Jesus' name, amen.

Whoever claims to love God yet hates a brother or sister is a liar.
For whoever does not love their brother and sister, whom they have seen,
cannot love God, whom they have not seen.
1 JOHN 4:20 NIV

Role Reversal

*D*ear Lord, when I was growing up, my parents seemed ageless. But I realize now that my time with them is getting shorter every day. They're getting older, Lord; and, more and more, I find myself looking out for them. This role reversal is really difficult for me. I'm accustomed to them looking out for me, and part of me wishes I could stay in their care for a while longer. Please give me strength to deal with this new phase of our relationship, and help me honor them as long as they live and beyond. Amen.

"Even to your old age, I am He, and even to gray hairs I will carry you! I have made, and I will bear; even I will carry, and will deliver you."
ISAIAH 46:4 NKJV

Shut the Door to Fear

*H*eavenly Father, help me recognize the presence of fear, and give me the courage to resist it by faith. I am Your child; I belong to You. Fear has no place in my life. Just as King David encouraged himself in the Lord, I encourage myself by remembering the great things You have done for me. I choose to keep fear out of my life like a homeowner keeps an intruder from breaking into his home.

For God has not given us a spirit of fear, but of power and of love and of a sound mind.
2 Timothy 1:7 NKJV

Spiritual Guardrails

Dear God, help me erect proper boundaries in my life. I don't want to fall prey to a sin simply because I wasn't being careful. Just like guardrails on a dangerous mountain highway, boundaries in my life keep me closer to center and farther away from the cliffs. I know Satan is plotting my destruction, but Your power is greater. Let me cooperate with Your grace through a careful lifestyle and a discerning spirit. In Christ's name, amen.

Stay alert! Watch out for your great enemy, the devil. He prowls around like a roaring lion, looking for someone to devour.
1 Peter 5:8 NLT

Passion and Purpose

Father, I'm in a rut. I like some familiarity, but this monotony is wearing away at my sense of purpose. I know there are parts of our lives that are not particularly glamorous, fulfilling, or significant (at least, on the surface). Yet living without passion or purpose isn't what You had in mind for us. Show me, Lord, how to find meaning in my everyday life. Open up my eyes to the subtle nuances of joy folded into life's mundane hours. I put my longings into Your hands. Amen.

In Him also we have obtained an inheritance, being predestined according to the purpose of Him who works all things according to the counsel of His will.
EPHESIANS 1:11 NKJV

Feeling Alone

Sometimes I feel alone and that nobody understands me. Even in the midst of people, I need Your comfort. Help me realize You are always with me.

I am convinced that nothing can ever separate us from God's love. Neither death nor life, neither angels nor demons, neither our fears for today nor our worries about tomorrow—not even the powers of hell can separate us from God's love. No power in the sky above or in earth below—indeed, nothing in all creation will ever be able to separate us from the love of God.
ROMANS 8:38–39 NLT

People at the Top

*D*ear God, I need help with my priorities. It is so easy for them to get out of whack. Show me the things I've let creep to the top that don't belong there. Point out to me those areas where I need to put more emphasis and commitment. Lord, let me remember that people are worth more than possessions and pursuits. Let my unseen checklist of priorities reflect that. Amen.

"For wherever your treasure is, you may be certain that your heart will be there too!"
MATTHEW 6:21 PHILLIPS

Quiet and Gentle

God, I read in Your Word that You value spirits that are gentle and quiet. At times, this is oh so hard for me, Lord! I'm not a total pushover, but I do have my own opinions about things. Sometimes it is so hard to keep quiet or speak softly. Yet, Lord, You know that I want to be that way. The universe has enough bossy women. Teach me, Lord, how to be quiet and gentle. Amen.

The unfading beauty of a gentle and quiet spirit. . .is of great worth in God's sight.
1 PETER 3:4 NIV

A Quiet Quest

Dear Lord, we all find great blessings when in the company of others, enjoying those times when we are with people. But I need Your help to embrace solitude, too. Let me see the value in spending some time alone, giving my mind time to decompress, refreshing my spirit in the quiet. Not only do I need to spend quiet time with You in personal worship, but also I need to incorporate into my daily routine those pockets of time when the music is off and the computer is down. Help me make times of quiet my quest. Amen.

"In quietness and confidence shall be your strength."
ISAIAH 30:15 NKJV

Lessons in Trust

Heavenly Father, teach me to trust. I know it's an area of weakness for me. In spite of the fact that I know Your character and Your track record, I find it so difficult to relinquish to You the important areas of life. Oh, I say that I will, and I do put forth effort to rely on You, but we both know that, in my heart, I find it hard to let You handle everything. So take my hand, Lord, and teach me to trust. You're the master; I am forever Your student. In Christ's name, amen.

I have put my trust in the Lord GOD, that I may declare all Your works.
PSALM 73:28 NKJV

Worry? Not!

*D*ear Lord, Your Word tells me it is wrong to worry. I try to tell myself that it's only concern, but actually, that's putting a nice spin on the issue. Older women used to say that females are just born worriers. I guess there's some truth to that, maybe because we're so invested in relationships and most of our worrying is about those we love and care for. Still, You know worry isn't good for us, and it doesn't accomplish anything. So, today, help me not worry, and turn all my "concerns" over to You.

Don't worry over anything whatever; tell God every detail of your needs in earnest and thankful prayer, and the peace of God which transcends human understanding, will keep constant guard over your hearts and minds as they rest in Christ Jesus.
Philippians 4:6–7 Phillips

The Simple Life

*D*ear God, *simplicity* is a buzz word today. It seems everyone wants "simple" in some fashion. Perhaps it's because life has become too complicated for many of us; we yearn for a more laidback lifestyle. Lord, I need to simplify my goals in my relationships and my work. Doing so will help me have a more laser-like focus. And in my spiritual life, a little simplifying might be good, too. Instead of daily reading numerous chapters of Your Word, help me concentrate on one or two verses, thus deepening my understanding of You. Lord, help me keep simple goals and a simple faith as I simply live for You. Amen.

Aspire to lead a quiet life, to mind your own business, and to work with your own hands.
1 Thessalonians 4:11 NKJV

The Path to Joy

❧❧❧

*L*ord, I live in a culture that demands more. Wherever I look, I see glossy advertising of things I "need." It's difficult to be content when you're bombarded with messages to the contrary. But I know that accumulating more stuff isn't the path to joy. And You don't bless me so I can indulge myself, but so I can share with others. Let my life be marked by restraint and a deep contentment that's rooted in You, the center of my fulfillment. In Jesus' name, amen.

Keep your lives free from the lust for money: be content with what you have.
HEBREWS 13:5 PHILLIPS

....

....

....

....

....

....

....

....

....

....

....

....

Resting on the Sabbath

*F*ather, You created us as beings that work and need rest. Sometimes I forget that. I get so caught up in all that must be accomplished. Slow my pace, Lord. Help me honor You by resting one day per week. Help me keep the Sabbath holy. Thank You for designing the week and for telling Your people to rest. It is up to me to follow Your command. Amen.

Remember the sabbath day, to keep it holy. Six days shalt thou labour,
and do all thy work: But the seventh day is the sabbath of the LORD thy God:
in it thou shalt not do any work.
EXODUS 20:8–10

Rest in the Lord

*H*eavenly Father, take my worries and burdens. I submit to You my anxieties. Fill me with the rest that calms my spirit when I trust in You. Sometimes I look at others' lives and compare them to my own. Why do they have what I desire? Especially when I know that they are not Christians! But You tell me not to be concerned with others' prosperity. I choose to rest in You. Amen.

Rest in the LORD, and wait patiently for him: fret not thyself because of him who prospereth in his way, because of the man who bringeth wicked devices to pass.
PSALM 37:7

Invitation to Rest

*J*esus, You told Your disciples to rest. You directed them to leave the crowd and to relax and eat. You saw that they had been busy with ministry, and they needed to recuperate. If You directed them to rest, even these twelve who worked at Your side daily, You must want me to rest as well. Remind me to take breaks from ministry. I needed to hear that You give me permission to rest! Amen.

And he said unto them, Come ye yourselves apart into a desert place, and rest a while: for there were many coming and going, and they had no leisure so much as to eat.

MARK 6:31

....

....

....

....

....

....

....

....

....

....

....

....

Still before the Lord

*F*ather, as I am still before You this morning, I focus on who You are. You are sovereign, all-knowing, and You have plans to prosper and not to harm me. You are the Prince of Peace, my provider, my protector, and my friend. You are holy and yet You draw near to me when I draw near to You. You are the one true God. And I worship You in the quiet of this morning. Amen.

Be still, and know that I am God: I will be exalted among the heathen, I will be exalted in the earth.
PSALM 46:10

Relaxation

Thank You, God, for the gift of relaxation. It is so nice to sit out on a patio in springtime or by the fireplace in winter and enjoy a good meal with friends or family. It is relaxing to my mind, my heart, and my spirit. Help me always set aside time for fellowship with others and to relax. Thank You for this blessing. Amen.

There is nothing better for a man, than that he should eat and drink, and that he should make his soul enjoy good in his labour. This also I saw, that it was from the hand of God. For who can eat, or who else can hasten hereunto, more than I?
ECCLESIASTES 2:24–25

Come to Jesus

I come to You, Lord Jesus. That is the first step. I come before You now in this quiet moment. As I begin this new day, calm my spirit. There is work that must be done today. But even as I work, I can find rest in You. Ease the tension and stress in me, Lord, as only You can do. Thank You for a sense of peace. Amen.

Come unto me, all ye that labour and are heavy laden, and I will give you rest.
MATTHEW 11:28

Calming the Storms

*L*ord, sometimes You calm storms, and other times You carry Your children through them. There is a storm raging in my heart. I ask that You end it, but I desire Your will for my life. If I must walk through this storm, will You go with me every step of the way? You are where my heart finds rest and peace, regardless of the outward circumstances. I love You, Lord. Amen.

And he arose, and rebuked the wind, and said unto the sea, Peace, be still.
And the wind ceased, and there was a great calm.
MARK 4:39

Finding Balance

*J*esus, when I think of Your ministry here on earth, I picture You teaching and casting out demons. You fed the five thousand and conversed with the woman at the well. You raised Lazarus from the dead! What a flurry of activity! But then I read that You slept. . .and during a storm that was frightening Your friends. If You rested, so shall I. I will set aside my work when it is appropriate to rest. Amen.

And, behold, there arose a great tempest in the sea, insomuch that the ship was covered with the waves: but he was asleep.
MATTHEW 8:24

Peaceful Sleep

*F*ather, thank You for the refreshment that sleep provides. I know it is Your desire that I rest after working all day. I will not fear the darkness of the night. I have nothing to be afraid of because You watch over me. Thank You for sweet, peaceful sleep. As I go about my day today, give me energy for the tasks at hand. And when evening comes, grant me rest again, I pray. Amen.

When thou liest down, thou shalt not be afraid: yea,
thou shalt lie down, and thy sleep shall be sweet.
PROVERBS 3:24

Slow to Speak

Father, I am often the opposite of what James 1:19-20 advises. I catch myself being quick to speak and slow to listen. I make assumptions and find out later I was wrong. I say things and later wish I had gotten all the facts first. Lord, I admit that this is not an easy task—being patient with those around me. Please put a guard over my tongue. Amen.

Wherefore, my beloved brethren, let every man be swift to hear, slow to speak, slow to wrath: For the wrath of man worketh not the righteousness of God.
JAMES 1:19−20

In Christ's Strength

*F*ather, I am so thankful for the strength that is mine as a Christian. I cannot do anything on my own, but through Christ, I can do all things. It is comforting to know that the word "all" includes the trials and concerns that I bring to You this morning. I lay them at Your feet, Lord. I take You at Your word. I can do all things through Jesus who lives in me. Amen.

I can do all things through Christ which strengtheneth me.
PHILIPPIANS 4:13

My Source of Strength

Father, at times I worry too much about what others think of me. Even when I just have a minor disagreement with a friend or coworker, I am afraid that the person will not like me anymore. I worry that I have not lived up to what was expected of me. Remind me, Father, that I must seek my ultimate strength and encouragement from You and You alone. Amen.

And David was greatly distressed; for the people spake of stoning him, because the soul of all the people was grieved, every man for his sons and for his daughters: but David encouraged himself in the LORD his God.
1 SAMUEL 30:6

God Is with Me

*H*eavenly Father, as I meet with You this morning, I find great strength in the knowledge that You will never leave me. Wherever I go, You are there with me. You are not just beside me, but You reside in my heart. I never have to be afraid. The Lord Almighty, the maker of heaven and earth, is with me. Thank You, Father, for the strength I find in You. Amen.

Have not I commanded thee? Be strong and of a good courage; be not afraid, neither be thou dismayed: for the LORD thy God is with thee whithersoever thou goest.

JOSHUA 1:9

Guidance in My Finances

*G*od, I ask for wisdom and guidance as I manage my finances. Help me plan ahead and set realistic goals. Teach me the difference between needs and wants—write it plainly upon my heart and mind. And then show me how to spend my time and money appropriately. As I grow in financial resources, direct me in knowing where the income should go.

*When his master saw that the L*ORD *was with him and that the L*ORD
gave him success in everything he did, Joseph found favor in his eyes.
GENESIS 39:3–4 NIV

Waiting Rooms

Dear Jesus, someone I love dearly is in the hospital. I'm sitting here in the busy waiting room, watching for the doctor, wanting news, and yet dreading to hear it. Others surround me, connected to this place by a person they care about. We're people from every stratum and season of life with one thing in common—knowing someone who is suffering physically. Lord, illness and injury have to obey Your will, and so do the emotions that burden the hearts of those here. Please visit every waiting area and patient's room and bring the cure that only comes from You—tranquility, mercy, and courage. Amen.

Now the God of peace be with you all.
ROMANS 15:33 NKJV

Every Gift Is from God

Everything I have comes from You. Remind me that I am only a custodian of Your gifts. I want to honor You, Lord, with my wealth. Help me put You first in everything I do. Never let me be deceived into believing that wealth provides me with happiness.

I know what it is to be in need, and I know what it is to have plenty. I have learned the secret of being content in any and every situation, whether well fed or hungry, whether living in plenty or in want.

PHILIPPIANS 4:12 NIV

Fitness

It's an exercise-crazy world we live in, Lord. Gym memberships are prized, morning jogs are eulogized, and workout clothing has become a fashion statement. There are some who make this area of self-care too important; they spend an inordinate amount of time on it. Yet others don't keep it high enough on their priority list. Help me, God, to keep the proper perspective of fitness, because, after all, I have a responsibility for the upkeep on this body. It's on loan from You. Amen.

Bodily fitness has a certain value, but spiritual fitness is essential both for this present life and for the life to come.
1 Timothy 4:8 Phillips

Endurance Required

*I*m finding, Lord, that the Christian life is one that requires endurance. It isn't enough to start well. So let me patiently and steadily move down the road to Christlikeness. I know difficulties will come; I've face some already. It reminds me of the words of the second verse of "Amazing Grace": "Through many dangers, toils and snares, I have already come. 'Tis grace that brought me safe thus far, and grace will lead me home." In Your name, amen.

Let us run with endurance the race that is set before us.
HEBREWS 12:1 NKJV

....

....

....

....

....

....

....

....

....

....

....

....

....

A Job for Me

*D*ear heavenly Father, I need a new job. You know the challenges I'm facing in my present situation. You understand the reasons why I need to make this change. There are so many people looking for work; employers have a large pool from which to draw. Still, You've promised to supply my basic needs if I would keep Your kingdom top priority in my life. So, I ask that You would direct my search and help me approach this transition with integrity and consideration for my present employer. I ask this in Your name, amen.

"But seek first the kingdom of God and His righteousness,
and all these things shall be added to you."
MATTHEW 6:33 NKJV

A Right Perspective of Money

*L*ord, help me look at money as something that serves me as I serve You. I refuse to let the things money can buy be a substitute for my relationship with You. Money will never make me happy or satisfy me. My attention and focus is on You, Lord. Help me never make a decision based on the pursuit of money, but help my heart forever pursue knowing You.

A good person leaves an inheritance for their children's children,
but a sinner's wealth is stored up for the righteous.
PROVERBS 13:22 NIV

For Creative Ideas

God, You are the Creator of the Universe. You knew every idea before it was thought by anyone. You understood every invention before it was dreamed up. Please give me creative ideas for ways to generate income. Help me be innovative in developing these ideas, and show me what You would have me do with them.

Careful planning puts you ahead in the long run;
hurry and scurry puts you further behind.
PROVERBS 21:5 MSG

Communication

Dear God, the Internet is a marvelous tool! Thank you for giving humankind the ability to invent it. But the Internet also has a great potential for evil. I ask You to protect my family from online predators, from sexual content, from sites that would have a negative influence on our relationship with You. Help me be prudent in my use of the web. Like any other means of communication, it can be used wrongly. But, with Your help, it can be an instrument for good in our home. Amen.

I will set nothing wicked before my eyes.
PSALM 101:3 NKJV

Real Relationships

$\mathcal{G}$od, I want to be real in my relationships. I want others to see You working in my life. Help me shift my focus from myself to those around me. I don't want my life to be consumed by empty religion and man-made rules. May my words be a reflection of a heart that is full of Your love and Your life.

These people make a big show of saying the right thing, but their heart isn't in it.
MATTHEW 15:8 MSG

Legitimate Faith

Lord, I don't want to fake it! I'm tired of saying one thing and doing another. Forgive me for pretending to have it all together. I don't want to be a wishy-washy Christian. Help me trust You and believe the promises You have given me in Your Word. I believe—help my unbelief.

So when you give to the needy, do not announce it with trumpets, as the hypocrites do in the synagogues and on the streets, to be honored by others. I tell you, they have received their reward in full.

MATTHEW 6:2 NIV

To Stay Connected

*G*od, there are so many distractions—so many things I feel I have to do. Help me stay connected to You throughout my day. I want to share it with You and be used by You to reach others. Speak to my heart and remind me that You have something for me to do today. Lead me by Your Spirit.

Walk by the Spirit, and you will not carry out the desire of the flesh.
GALATIANS 5:16 NASB

Natural Consequences

*D*ear Lord, I know You've forgiven me for that horrible wrong. I thought when I repented that would take care of things, but I'm learning that the natural consequences still hurt. I know they won't disappear, but I pray that You will use them in a positive way—perhaps to keep others from making the same mistake. Amen.

Blessed is he whose transgression is forgiven, whose sin is covered.
PSALM 32:1

I Blew It

*L*ord, I blew it today. I was unkind to my family. I wish I could take back my attitude and words. Sometimes it's difficult for me to understand why You still love me. I am so thankful You would trust me with a family, even though I've done a pretty terrible job of nurturing today. Please forgive me. Your Word promises me cleansing if I confess. Help me remember this the next time I feel frustrated and impatient. Help me exercise my will and choose to respond appropriately to the family You've given me. In Christ's name, amen.

*If we confess our sins, He is faithful and just to forgive us our sins
and to cleanse us from all unrighteousness.*
1 John 1:9 NKJV

Cherish

*D*ear God, thank You for sending a strong man to love me. He is strong not only in physical strength, but in his emotional and mental stability as well. I don't want that to change, but I ask You to help him learn the language of tenderness. I understand it's hard for a man to grasp what affection and gentle words mean to a woman, but I ask You to help my husband learn how to cherish me verbally. And there may be some significant need in his life that I am not meeting—give me insight and let me make his happiness my goal. Amen.

Love knows no limit to its endurance, no end to its trust,
no fading of its hope; it can outlast anything.
1 CORINTHIANS 13:7 PHILLIPS

....

....

....

....

....

....

....

....

....

....

....

....

For Boldness in Ministry

Lord, I don't know where to start in sharing my faith with others. When You give me the opportunity, help me realize You are opening the door. Help me recognize Your timing and follow Your leading. Speak to me and through me. Give me Your words that will touch others' hearts and turn them toward a relationship with You.

I am not ashamed of the gospel, because it is the power of God for the salvation of everyone who believes: first to the Jew, then to the Gentile.

ROMANS 1:16 NIV

Lord, Carry My Friend

My friend is hurting, dear Jesus. She's had so many struggles in her life lately, and she feels like she's about to hit rock bottom. I've tried to be there for her, but right now she needs You in a special way. Please let her know that You want to carry her through this trial. Help her to trust You. Amen.

A friend loveth at all times.
PROVERBS 17:17

True Homeland Perspective

*G*od, I want to live with an eternal perspective. Heaven is more than a feel-good fable for the graveside. It's an actual place, as real as this earth and far more lasting. When I live like this earth is the ultimate goal, I tend toward selfish indulgence. When I remember that heaven is my real destination, I put value on the lasting things, the things of true importance. Remind me to keep an eye toward Your heavenly kingdom. Amen.

They freely admitted that they lived on this earth as exiles and foreigners. Men who say that mean, of course, that their eyes are fixed upon their true home-land.
Hebrews 11:13–14 Phillips

Time Management

*D*ear God, sometimes I think I need more than twenty-four hours in my day! It seems I never have enough time. I think with longing about simpler seasons in my life when I could actually complete my to-do lists. There was such satisfaction in having a few stress-free moments. Now my schedule is filled, and I'm so harried. Holy Spirit, please guide me in this area of my life. How I use my time is part of stewardship, so I'm asking for Your wisdom. Show me how to manage the hours I have so I can honor You in everything I do. In Christ's name, amen.

Teach us to number our days, that we may gain a heart of wisdom.
PSALM 90:12 NIV

Meekness

*H*eavenly Father, I want to develop the characteristic of meekness, a kind of quiet strength. Rather than a sign of a pushover, meekness is a trait of the strong. It takes guts to be silent when you want to speak. Meekness is not a goal for the weak of heart. It is, rather, for those who would be in the forefront of spiritual growth. Like Moses, the meekest man on earth (see Numbers 12:3), we can reap the rewards of quiet strength in our lives. Amen.

With all lowliness and meekness, with longsuffering, forbearing one another in love.
EPHESIANS 4:2

Back to Center

*H*eavenly Father, I need balance in my life. It's one of the hardest things for humans to achieve. We're so prone to lopsidedness, to extremes. Maintaining center is challenging. That's why I need You to straighten me out and help me stay in the narrow way. In those areas of my life where I'm listing to the side, bring me back to center, O Lord. In Jesus' name, amen.

Don't wander away from the path but forge steadily onward. On the right path the limping foot recovers strength and does not collapse.
HEBREWS 12:13 PHILLIPS

When Others Are Watching

*I*t's hard to be an example, Lord. I don't do everything the way I know I should. I want to be strong and diligent to do what is right. Help me hold fast to my convictions. Help me be honest when I make mistakes. I want to encourage others by following You faithfully. Give me courage and strength to live my life to please You so I can say to them, "Follow me, as I follow Christ."

Be an example to the believers with your words, your actions, your love, your faith, and your pure life.
1 TIMOTHY 4:12 NCV

Legacy

*D*ear God, what kind of legacy am I leaving? I want to be remembered as more than a woman who dressed nicely, had a great family, and went to church. I want to be remembered for the way I invested myself in the lives of others. After all, love is the only lasting thing on this earth, something that will remain when I am physically gone but living with You in eternity. Lord, let my legacy be wrapped up in serving others in love. In Jesus' name, amen.

Prophecy and speaking in unknown languages and special knowledge will become useless. But love will last forever!

1 Corinthians 13:8 nlt

Keeping My Two Cents

Father, You created me with an opinion about everything. I make the mistake of thinking that people value my opinion. Help me keep my opinions to myself and instead share what You want me to say. Use me, Lord, to speak Your Word and Your wisdom into their lives. Remind me that I am to be about my Father's business. I want to be ready to speak a word at the right time—but only if that Word comes from You.

Keep your tongue from speaking evil and your lips from telling lies!
PSALM 34:13 NLT

Inside and Out

God, I want to live from the inside out. I want people to experience the real me every time we meet. Help me examine the values that direct my life. Help me know what I believe and why I believe it. You know the things I struggle with. Give me Your grace and strength as I learn and grow in those areas. I want to honor You in everything I do.

Provide people with a glimpse of good living and of the living God.
PHILIPPIANS 2:15 MSG

....

....

....

....

....

....

....

....

....

....

....

....

....

....

To Know You, Lord

*H*eavenly Father, I am Your child. I belong to You. I want to know You more. Give me an understanding of who You are and what You are like. Teach me the things that are important to You so they can become important to me. Help me put You first in my life. Give me wisdom to choose time with You and to eliminate distractions that keep me too busy for You.

I want you to show love, not offer sacrifices. I want you to know me more than I want burnt offerings.
HOSEA 6:6 NLT

To Know the Truth

Lord, thank You for making absolute truth available. You came into the world to testify for truth. It is not relative to what I think or feel. Truth is objective and is based on Your Word, the Bible. Help me to know the truth and see it clearly in my life.

We know also that the Son of God has come and has given us understanding,
so that we may know him who is true. And we are in him who is true by being
in his Son Jesus Christ. He is the true God and eternal life.

1 JOHN 5:20 NIV

Discovering Leadership

*H*eavenly Father, I want to understand how to become a leader. Jesus led by serving others. He gave of Himself freely to show us the way to truth. Teach me what it takes to lead as I begin by following You and the leaders You placed in my life. Give me a heart to serve and the patience to not take shortcuts in the lessons You want me to learn.

It is senseless to pay tuition to educate a fool, since he has no heart for learning.
PROVERBS 17:16 NLT

The Power of Wisdom

Father, I am listening to Your instruction. I will hide Your Word in my heart, and I will not forget what You have done for me. I want to experience Your blessings. I will keep Your commandments, not just because You said to, but because I love You. Give me Your wisdom, Lord. Help me gain understanding.

They won't go to school to learn about me, or buy a book called God in Five Easy Lessons. They'll all get to know me firsthand, the little and the big, the small and the great.
HEBREWS 8:11 MSG

Passionate in Prayer

*F*ather, I realize prayer is important for building a strong relationship with You. Jesus prayed constantly and consistently. People in relationships talk to one another. I never want to neglect my relationship with You. Help me be faithful to You in prayer. I want to be open to hearing Your voice at all times.

A good person produces good things from the treasury of a good heart, and an evil person produces evil things from the treasury of an evil heart. What you say flows from what is in your heart.
LUKE 6:45 NLT

Developing a Passion for the Bible

Father, help me make daily Bible study as much a part of my life as eating. Remind me that the Bible is more than a book, that it contains words revealing Your love for me. Holy Spirit, speak to my heart and tell me what I need to discover each day. Bring what I've read back to my memory so I can meditate on what Your Word is saying to me personally.

Draw near to God and He will draw near to you. Cleanse your hands,
you sinners; and purify your hearts, you double-minded.
JAMES 4:8 NASB

The Same Old Me

*L*ord, today I come to You a bit discouraged. The traits I see in myself are ones I don't like. It seems I could do much more for You without some of the inherent flaws of my personality. So help me overcome my defects or use me in spite of them. Help me love myself, as imperfect as I am, and strive to be the best me I can be. I know You can find a way around my impediments and use me for Your glory, just like You used Moses in spite of his speech problem. Amen.

You have searched me, LORD, and you know me.
PSALM 139:1 NIV

Good Enough

Father, shopping for clothing at the mall makes me so insecure. The store windows are filled with posters of glamorous women in size zero clothing. I feel I will never "measure up" to these air-brushed supermodels. Like every other twenty-first century woman I know, I struggle with body image. Although these feelings of inferiority seem petty and a bit self-centered, they are so real sometimes that I get depressed. I know that isn't what You want for me. Help me with these feelings and show me the way to triumph over them. In Christ's name, amen.

I praise you because I am fearfully and wonderfully made.
PSALM 139:14 NIV

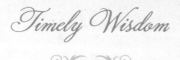

Timely Wisdom

Lord, I wasted my time this afternoon watching a movie. I needed to do other things, but I got caught up in the plot. Now I'm running behind in my schedule. Thank You, Lord, for giving writers and moviemakers the gifts necessary to craft moving stories, sometimes life-changing dramas. But help me use my time more wisely so I can enjoy this pleasure sans guilt. And, Lord, help me guard my mind carefully when I'm selecting what to watch. Amen.

For the LORD gives wisdom; from His mouth come knowledge and understanding.
PROVERBS 2:6 NKJV

No Spirit of Fear

Father, I deal with a phobia. It isn't anything life threatening, but it's embarrassing. I haven't told anyone, and I'm hoping I never have to. But I ask You now to help me; I don't want my phobia to keep me from living the life You've planned for me. Help me bring this fear to You; show me that You are in control, that You are the security system in my life. I ask this in Jesus' name, amen.

I sought the LORD, and he heard me, and delivered me from all my fears.
PSALM 34:4

Fixing My Thoughts

God, today I'm having a pity party. My thoughts are so focused on earthly things that I am having trouble looking up. I could mope around here all day, but I guess it's time for the music to stop and the party to end. Lord, You can't work through me when I'm feeling sorry for myself. Forgive me for my pettiness and let me respond to life with maturity. Help me focus on good, praiseworthy things. In Christ's name, amen.

Fix your thoughts on what is true, and honorable,
and right, and pure, and lovely, and admirable.
PHILIPPIANS 4:8 NLT

Strength to Combat Temptation

God, at times I sink so deep into temptation that I forget Your promise. You have said that there is always a way out, a way of escape. You have promised in Your Word that nothing is strong enough to separate me from Your love. I confess to You this morning that temptation is alive and well in my heart. Set my eyes on the way of escape. Free me from temptation, I pray. Amen.

There hath no temptation taken you but such as is common to man: but God is faithful, who will not suffer you to be tempted above that ye are able; but will with the temptation also make a way to escape, that ye may be able to bear it.

1 Corinthians 10:13

Mountain-Moving Faith

I cannot imagine, Jesus, that anything I could do would compare to Your works. But You taught, when you were here on earth, that there is great strength in faith. On more than one occasion You told Your followers that they could do greater things even than You had done. The source? Faith. Give me that type of faith, Lord. The type of faith that moves mountains! Amen.

Jesus answered and said unto them, Verily I say unto you, If ye have faith, and doubt not, ye shall not only do this which is done to the fig tree, but also if ye shall say unto this mountain, Be thou removed, and be thou cast into the sea; it shall be done.

MATTHEW 21:21

Fear No Evil

*H*ow wonderful, God, that death has no power over the Christian! You are a strong and mighty God, the one true God. You are with me, protecting me all the way. And when the end of this life comes, whenever that may be, You will walk with me through the valley of the shadow of death. Death has lost its sting because Christ has conquered it! In Your name I pray, amen.

---

*Yea, though I walk through the valley of the shadow of death, I will fear no evil:
for thou art with me; thy rod and thy staff they comfort me.*
PSALM 23:4

A Spirit of Power

*G*od, a spirit of fear is not from You! It is from the enemy. I choose to believe the promise from Your Word that You have given believers a spirit of power, love, and a sound mind. I will go about my day with strength. I will love others well. I will make solid and right decisions based on Your living Word. I claim this promise. You are my strength! Amen.

For God hath not given us the spirit of fear; but of power,
and of love, and of a sound mind.

2 TIMOTHY 1:7

My Strength and My Song

Lord, You don't just provide my strength. You ARE my strength. Through You I am able to do all things. At times I forget this. I lean on my own strength, which is never enough. It always fails me. Today I will stand firm on my foundation, which is salvation through Christ. I will find my strength in the one true God. I will worship You with my life. Amen.

The LORD is my strength and song, and he is become my salvation: he is my God, and I will prepare him an habitation; my father's God, and I will exalt him.
EXODUS 15:2

Sharing the Good News

Why do I find it so hard just to open my mouth and share the Gospel? Give me strength, Lord, to share the good news of Jesus with others. When the opportunity presents itself, even today, I ask that You will give me strength to share openly. The world needs You. I have received the Good News, and it is my responsibility to spread the word. Empower me, I pray. In Your name, amen.

Notwithstanding the Lord stood with me, and strengthened me; that by me the preaching might be fully known, and that all the Gentiles might hear: and I was delivered out of the mouth of the lion.

2 TIMOTHY 4:17

He Is Strong

*G*od, please show Yourself strong in my time of need! I need your strength today. Just as the song says, "I am weak, but You are strong." I am so thankful for that exception today. "But You are strong." I will cling to that. When I am at my very weakest, when there seems to be no way I can face the future, I will face it in Your strength. Show Yourself strong in my life. In Jesus' name, amen.

For the eyes of the LORD run to and fro throughout the whole earth,
to shew himself strong in the behalf of them whose heart is perfect toward him.
2 CHRONICLES 16:9

He Increases My Strength

*A*ll I have ever known is this body, Father. All I know is becoming weary. This body grows weak at times. But You are different. You never grow tired. You don't sleep or look away. Your eye is always upon my life. Your strength is consistent and eternal. Renew my strength, Lord. I need physical and spiritual power to live in this world. Thank You for strengthening me! Amen.

He giveth power to the faint; and to them that have no might he increaseth strength.
Even the youths shall faint and be weary, and the young men shall utterly fall: But they
that wait upon the LORD *shall renew their strength; they shall mount up with wings as*
eagles; they shall run, and not be weary; and they shall walk, and not faint.
ISAIAH 40:29–31

Confidence in the Lord

Lord, I admit it. Sometimes I am afraid. I feel helpless. My mind runs wild with anxiety. Thank You for the promise that through Christ, this is not my norm. Certainly at times in my humanity, I cower before an unknown future or feel defeated by the pressures of today. But You have given me a spirit of power and love. You have given me a sound mind. I find my confidence in You, God. Amen.

The LORD is my light and my salvation; whom shall I fear?
The LORD is the strength of my life; of whom shall I be afraid?
PSALM 27:1

God Knows Me

God, the Bible says that You knew me even before I was formed in my mother's womb. I find confidence in this. You have been with me all along this journey! As I face this day, help me remember that I am never alone. You go before me to prepare the future. You walk with me through the present. And You were there with me since before I was born. Wow! Amen.

For thou hast possessed my reins: thou hast covered me in my mother's womb.
I will praise thee; for I am fearfully and wonderfully made: marvellous are
thy works; and that my soul knoweth right well.
PSALM 139:13–14

Taking a Stand

There is nothing in this world that can separate me from Your love! Father, what strength I find in this promise! As a Christian, I stand out. At times, no one agrees with the stand I take or the choices I make. Sometimes it feels like the whole world is on the other side! Thank You that You are always with me. I face this day with confidence because You are on my side. Amen.

Though an host should encamp against me, my heart shall not fear:
though war should rise against me, in this will I be confident.
PSALM 27:3

Facing the Future

*L*ord, thank You that I don't have to worry about tomorrow. I can face an uncertain future with a certain God at my side. You are all the confidence I need! You have never left me and You never will. Tomorrow may bring a scary diagnosis, an unthinkable loss, or a deep disappointment. But You will be there holding my hand. You can take care of me through any storm. I love You, Lord. Amen.

Take therefore no thought for the morrow: for the morrow shall take thought for the things of itself. Sufficient unto the day is the evil thereof.
MATTHEW 6:34

Wisdom from God

$\mathcal{F}$ather, the world does not have wisdom to offer me. True wisdom comes only from You. Help me today to walk as a wise daughter of the sovereign King of kings. Keep me from the temptation to listen to what the world calls wisdom. Even in times such as these, there is a remnant of Your people. We will be known by our love and by the wisdom we possess. Amen.

See then that ye walk circumspectly, not as fools, but as wise,
redeeming the time, because the days are evil.
EPHESIANS 5:15—16

Wise Counsel

*H*elp me, Lord, to know when I need to seek counsel from others. I don't want to step out, as I sometimes have in the past, on my own. I want to walk in Your ways and in Your will. Sometimes we all need help. Guide me to someone who is grounded in Your Word so that any counsel I receive will be truth. Give me wisdom, I pray. Amen.

The way of a fool is right in his own eyes: but he that hearkeneth unto counsel is wise.
PROVERBS 12:15

Applying Instruction

God, give me ears to hear. Sharpen my senses and make me wise. I am often proud. I think I know it all. But I don't. I need instruction from You. I know this comes in many forms. . .through reading and meditating on Your Word, through Your people, and through circumstances. Help me be a good listener and apply the instruction You send my way. I want to be wise, Father. Amen.

Hear counsel, and receive instruction, that thou mayest be wise in thy latter end.
PROVERBS 19:20

When to Remain Silent

Heavenly Father, Your Word says that the tongue has great power. My words can help or harm. There are times when silence is best. Help me to know the difference between times I should speak and times I should keep still. I pray for wisdom as I go through this day. I want my speech to honor You. Put a guard over my lips, I pray. Amen.

In the multitude of words there wanteth not sin: but he that refraineth his lips is wise.
PROVERBS 10:19

A Wise Woman

*G*od, others look to me as an example. I am a leader whether I want to be or not. I set the tone in my home. Give me grace and patience. Teach me how to build a home with a strong foundation rather than one that collapses when the storms come. Make my resistance strong against Satan, who tempts me to argue and isolate. Instead find me to be a peacemaker in my home. Amen.

Every wise woman buildeth her house: but the foolish plucketh it down with her hands.
PROVERBS 14:1

A Calm Spirit

ℒord Jesus, I read in the Bible of the times that You expressed anger. They were few and far between. It was a righteous anger, a godly anger over great offenses to Your Father. I, on the other hand, sometimes have a short fuse. I want to be wise. "Fool" is a strong word. Your Word says that to have a hot temper is foolish. Replace my anger with even-tempered responses, I pray. Amen.

A fool uttereth all his mind: but a wise man keepeth it in till afterwards.
PROVERBS 29:11

Godly Wisdom

*L*ord, there are so many self-help books out there now. There are even therapists on TV who claim to have all the answers for our problems. Not to mention the opinions of my friends and family members! I read in Your Word that You were the one who put the wisdom in Solomon's heart. Open my eyes that I may see. I want the wisdom of God Almighty. Grant me wisdom, I pray. Amen.

*And all the kings of the earth sought the presence of Solomon,
to hear his wisdom, that God had put in his heart.*
2 CHRONICLES 9:23

Hospitality

Dear Lord, I need to improve my skills in hospitality. Because You have blessed me, I need to share with others. In fact, hospitality is one of those virtues the apostle Paul commanded of the church. Sharing my home with others is my Christian duty and also a great way to reach out to the unbelievers I have befriended. Please let me not dread hosting others, but rather find ways to make it doable and enjoyable for all. In Jesus' name, amen.

Use hospitality one to another without grudging.
1 Peter 4:9

The Real Me

Heavenly Father, so many people in my world wear masks. We earth-dwellers are afraid to be real with others; we fear losing the respect and esteem of our peers. And, oddly enough, we're often afraid to be real with even You—and You know everything about us anyway. I want to be genuine in my approach and interaction with others, including You. Give me the courage to reject the lure of artificial "perfectness" and instead live out my life and relationships in a real way. Amen.

I have chosen the way of truth.
PSALM 119:30 NKJV

Friends for Every Need

Dear Heavenly Father, I am grateful for my friends. They are such a vital part of my life. When my family can't be there, my friends come through for me. When I need someone to gripe to, they will listen. When I need a kick to get me going again, they don't hesitate. My journey through life would be so lonely and unhappy without these amazing women who walk it with me. Thank You for blessing me through them. Help me return the favor. Amen.

A time to weep, and a time to laugh; a time to mourn, and a time to dance.
ECCLESIASTES 3:4 NKJV

Moving and Making Friends

*G*od, I don't like change or new places. I'd rather just stay in my comfort zone. But that's not happening. Here I am in a strange new environment. I miss my old friends so much. I feel like crying just thinking about them. But that won't do any good, will it? I need some heavenly moxie. It's time to square my shoulders, walk in, smile, introduce myself, and meet some new people. I guess I can think of them as pre-friends. Help me not to chicken out! Thank You. Amen.

A man who has friends must himself be friendly.
PROVERBS 18:24 NKJV

A Model of Modesty

Dear Father, there is a lot of talk in the Christian women's community about modesty. It's an issue that really goes counter to our culture. Fashion today is more about being "hot" than anything else. Clothing often seems to reveal more than it covers. Yet, God, I don't want the way I dress to send out a message that contradicts my relationship with You. Let me remember that attracting attention to my body puts the focus on me, not You. And that my dressing immodestly could be a source of struggle for my brothers in Christ. Modesty can be tasteful and beautiful; help me model it. Amen.

I desire therefore that. . .women adorn themselves in modest apparel. . .which is proper for women professing godliness, with good works.
1 TIMOTHY 2:8–10 NKJV

Fadeless Beauty

Dear God, I'm getting older. That's not news to You, I know. You've seen my journey from day one. But now my body is revolting and my hormones are rebelling. I don't like looking in the mirror because it shocks me to see lines on my face. Inside I don't feel old, but my body doesn't agree. Still, Lord, help me remember that my identity in You is changeless and my beauty in You is fadeless. The magazines may say differently, but I know that in Your sight, I have a loveliness that time can't touch. Amen.

The unfading loveliness of a calm and gentle spirit,
a thing very precious in the eyes of God.
1 Peter 3:4 Phillips

What Pleases God

*G*od, I want to be passionate about the purpose You have for me. Show me the things in my life that please You and give me the courage and strength to pursue those things. Keep my purpose before me, fill my heart, and give me right motives to accomplish all You have set before me. As long as You are with me and my focus is on what pleases You, I cannot fail.

How much more shall the blood of Christ, who through the eternal Spirit offered Himself without spot to God, cleanse your conscience from dead works to serve the living God?
HEBREWS 9:14 NKJV

For a Restored Soul

*L*ord, in pursuit of what I thought should be my passion, my soul has been wounded. I am here to ask You for encouragement and strength. I'm not a quitter, but I need to make some major heart adjustments. Guide me with Your Word and speak to me through preaching and teaching. Show me how to ask for help, and bring people who love me and Your Word into my life to give me godly counsel.

He restores my soul; He leads me in the paths of righteousness for His name's sake.
PSALM 23:3 NKJV

....

....

....

....

....

....

....

....

....

....

....

....

....

Coveting

God, it's so easy to break the tenth commandment: Do not covet (see Exodus 20:17). Coveting is a way of life for many in our world. But You say we shouldn't compare ourselves with the "Joneses," nor envy them and what they have. Whatever You've given me is to be enjoyed and received, not held up for inspection. Teach me a deeper gratefulness for Your blessings. In Jesus' name, amen.

Let your conduct be without covetousness.
HEBREWS 13:5 NKJV

Golden Words Needed

Heavenly Father, today I need affirming words. You know that words are important to me as a woman. You also know that I struggle with self-worth. The other people in my world don't always meet my need to be affirmed verbally, and I can't expect them to fulfill every void in my life. So, Lord, let me look to and in Your Word to find the love and encouragement I need. In Jesus' name, amen.

A word fitly spoken is like apples of gold in settings of silver.
Proverbs 25:11 NKJV

Poise

*H*eavenly Father, I need poise—that kind of gracious manner and behavior that characterized women of past generations. It seems to be disdained in my culture. Women now are expected and encouraged to be free spirits—unrestricted by convention and decorum. But I cringe when I observe women using crude language, slouching in their seats, and adopting careless ways of walking and eating. I don't want to seem prissy and uppity, but I do want to guard against being too informal. Help me develop the traits that portray womanhood as the gentle, beautiful, fascinating gender You designed. Amen.

Like a gold ring in a pig's snout is a beautiful woman who shows no discretion.
PROVERBS 11:22 NIV

Fear of the Lord

Lord, there is no greater one than You. I come before You this morning as Your daughter and yet, I must not let the fact that You are my Abba Father (Daddy) negate Your holiness. You are set apart. You are good. You are all that I am not in my humanity. I am humbled, and I revere You. May my fear of the Lord be the beginning of wisdom in my spirit. Amen.

And unto man he said, Behold, the fear of the LORD, that is wisdom;
and to depart from evil is understanding.
JOB 28:28

Right Paths

The right path is often the one less traveled. I am learning this, Father, oh so slowly. You will always lead me in the right path. You will never lead me astray. I have been at the crossroads many times, and I will face such choices again and again. Keep my heart focused on You that I might be led down pleasant paths, paths that will glorify my King. Amen.

I have taught thee in the way of wisdom; I have led thee in right paths.

PROVERBS 4:11

God's Counsel Is Eternal

Lord, I wish my heart was always in tune with Yours. I wish that I did not experience temptations to stray from Your perfect plan. But in truth, I struggle. There is a force within me that is fleshly and human. I feel pulled in the wrong direction at times. I know that Your counsel is eternal. It is a strong foundation on which I want to build my life. Strengthen me, I pray. Amen.

There are many devices in a man's heart; nevertheless the counsel of the LORD, that shall stand.
PROVERBS 19:21

....

....

....

....

....

....

....

....

....

....

....

....

....

....

Grant Me Wisdom

Lord, give me wisdom. I ask for wisdom from the one true God, the wise one, the all-knowing, omnipotent One. You are the giver of all knowledge. You are the way, the truth, and the life. In You, I find the answers to life's puzzling questions. I seek You and I find You. As I meditate upon Your Word, instruct me, I pray. I ask these things in Jesus' name, amen.

And God gave Solomon wisdom and understanding exceeding much, and largeness of heart, even as the sand that is on the sea shore. And Solomon's wisdom excelled the wisdom of all the children of the east country, and all the wisdom of Egypt.
1 Kings 4:29–30

Grace with Others

Jesus, You came to earth to live among us. You were fully God and yet fully man. You were, as the book of John says, full of grace and truth. May I follow Your example. May I be found full of grace and truth. Give me a gracious, forgiving spirit. Grant me the discernment to see Your truth, Your light—even amidst the darkness of the world. Thank You, Lord. Amen.

And the Word was made flesh, and dwelt among us, (and we beheld his glory, the glory as of the only begotten of the Father,) full of grace and truth.
JOHN 1:14

A Messenger of Grace

Lord, make me a messenger of grace and peace. When I enter a room and when I leave it, may grace and peace be the mark that I was there. Season my conversations with these positive elements. Remove all malice and gossip from my thoughts and speech. Help me be more like Jesus. I want to be a peacemaker. I want to be known as gracious. Amen.

Grace be to you and peace from God our Father, and from the Lord Jesus Christ.
2 CORINTHIANS 1:2

Hope for the Future

Lord, I can't see the future. I see only one piece of the puzzle at a time, but You see the finished product. As I go through this day, I will not fear because You are in control. When things seem hopeless, there is hope. My hope is in a Sovereign God who says He knows the plans He has for me. I am counting on You to see me through. Amen.

For I know the thoughts that I think toward you, saith the LORD,
thoughts of peace, and not of evil, to give you an expected end.
JEREMIAH 29:11

Finding Hope in Scripture

*T*hank You, heavenly Father, for Your holy Word. The scriptures, which were inspired by You and written long ago, remain today. As I read and meditate upon scripture today, I ask that You would fill me with hope. Comfort me through Your Word. Encourage my spirit. Strengthen me for the tasks that lay ahead of me today. And instruct me in the ways You would have me go. Amen.

For whatsoever things were written aforetime were written for our learning, that we through patience and comfort of the scriptures might have hope.
ROMANS 15:4

....

....

....

....

....

....

....

....

....

....

....

....

....

Reason to Hope

God, this world seems hopeless. People let me down. They are only human. I let them down as well. Life brings disappointments and rejections. I am thankful that You are faithful and true. You are not like men and women. What You say You will do, You always do. You are true to Your Word. You have said that I am your child and that You will never leave me. You are my hope! Amen.

God is not a man, that he should lie; neither the son of man, that he should repent: hath he said, and shall he not do it? or hath he spoken, and shall he not make it good?

Numbers 23:19

Showing That I Love God

How do I show that I love You, God? It must be more than merely a phrase I use in prayer. The way I show it is by keeping Your commandments. I need Your strength for this. I fail every day. Renew my desire to live according to Your principles. They are not suggestions. They are commands. Honoring them will cause me to see You at work in my life. I love You, Lord. Amen.

He that hath my commandments, and keepeth them, he it is that loveth me:
and he that loveth me shall be loved of my Father, and I will love him,
and will manifest myself to him.
JOHN 14:21

Amazing Grace

Lord, I get so caught up in trying to do good works sometimes. I need to remember that I am saved by grace. You are pleased with me simply because I believe in Your Son, Jesus, and I have accepted Him as my Savior. You do not bless me or withhold good gifts based on my performance. Remind me of Your amazing grace, and make me gracious with others. In Jesus' name I pray, amen.

For by grace are ye saved through faith; and that not of yourselves: it is the gift of God: not of works, lest any man should boast.
EPHESIANS 2:8–9

Harmful Relationships

*L*ord, I generally think of relationships as being between people, and I fail to remember that my relationship to things can seriously affect how I react to people. For instance, sometimes I get so involved in a television show that I fail to give needed attention to my family. Forgive me, Father. Be in charge of my relationships. Amen.

And beside this, giving all diligence, add to your faith virtue; and to virtue knowledge; and to knowledge temperance; and to temperance patience; and to patience godliness; and to godliness brotherly kindness; and to brotherly kindness charity.
2 Peter 1:5–7

Steward of Grace

*T*hank You for the gifts You have given me, Lord. I look around at the other believers in my life. We are all gifted in different ways. Help me be a good steward of the gifts You have entrusted me with in this life. Instead of looking out for myself, may I have opportunities to use my abilities to minister to others. I understand that it is in doing so that I honor You. Amen.

As every man hath received the gift, even so minister the same one to another, as good stewards of the manifold grace of God.
1 Peter 4:10

An Heir to the King

*H*eavenly Father, thank You for adopting me as an heir to the King of kings! You provided a way for me to come before You, holy God. Christ carried my sin as His burden. It was nailed to the cross and has been forgiven forever, once and for all. Thank You for the abundant life that is mine because I am Yours. I praise You for viewing me through a lens called grace. Amen.

That being justified by his grace, we should be made heirs according to the hope of eternal life.
TITUS 3:7

Loving My Enemies

*L*ord, some of Your commands are easy to understand, such as taking care of widows and orphans. But some of them go against human nature. It's easier to show mercy to those we love, but You tell us to love our enemies. You command us to love those who are hard to love. Give me a love for the unlovable, Father. I want to have a heart that pleases You. Amen.

For if ye love them which love you, what reward have ye? do not even the publicans the same? And if ye salute your brethren only, what do ye more than others? do not even the publicans so?

Matthew 5:46–47

All I Need

Heavenly Father, You are a God of hope, joy, and great love. I don't need signs or wonders. I often wait for people or situations to turn from hopeless to hopeful. But my hope is in You. I need not wait for anything else or look for some other source. I quiet myself before You this morning and ask that You renew the hope within my heart. Thank You, Father. Amen.

And now, Lord, what wait I for? my hope is in thee.
PSALM 39:7

Gossip

*L*ord, I got caught in gossip today. I didn't mean to, though. A group of us were just talking about this and that, and You know how women are. We're so into relationships and what others are doing. Before long, the conversation had dug itself a little too deep into someone else's life. I tried to stop listening but didn't try hard enough. By the time we broke up our little gabfest, I felt terribly guilty. Please forgive me, Father. Give me the courage to make the right decision next time; help me refuse to listen to negative stories about individuals who are not there to defend themselves. In Jesus' name, amen.

Let all. . .evil speaking be put away from you, with all malice.
EPHESIANS 4:31 NKJV

Music

Dear Lord, music is the universal language of the human family. Today, music is available on a multitude of electronic devices. And there are so many genres—an array of listening options. Some appeal to me; others don't. But I want to base my choices on Your principles. What I listen to will affect my mood, my attitude, and my spiritual state of being. Holy Spirit, give me discernment. Let the music to which I listen not go counter to what You're trying to do in me. Amen.

Whatsoever ye do, do all to the glory of God.

1 Corinthians 10:31

To-Do Lists

God, I like to know what's coming up next in my life. I like to chart the items requiring some kind of action from me. To-do lists are my way of planning out the day and week. The lists keep me on track, but anything can be detrimental if it becomes too important. Help me avoid plotting and planning my life so completely that there is no room for divine interruptions, for Providence to intervene. Give me patience with those who cause my day to go awry; let me see beyond the irritation to what You have in mind. In Jesus' name, amen.

We can make our plans, but the LORD determines our steps.
PROVERBS 16:9 NLT

Anger

*G*od, I need a solution for my anger. Sometimes I let it take over, then end up regretting what it leads me to say or do. As I pray and study and grow closer to You, show me ways to control it. Guide me to the right verses to memorize and incorporate into my life. Lead me to someone who can keep me accountable. And, most of all, help me strive for self-control. Amen.

If it is possible, as much as depends on you, live peaceably with all men. Beloved, do not avenge yourselves, but rather give place to wrath; for it is written, "Vengeance is Mine, I will repay," says the Lord.

Romans 12:18–19 nkjv

Father, peace is an elusive emotion. So many people talk about peace, but few can claim it. You promised to give us Your peace, a calm assurance that You are present and sovereign in all our ways. I want more of this peace every day. Although there are many upsetting things in my world, Your peace will help me cope with them all. Amid Your peace, I am neither troubled nor afraid, merely allowing myself to bask in Your presence. Amen.

"Peace I leave with you, My peace I give to you."
JOHN 14:27 NKJV

De-Stress

Lord, because it has become so overused, the word *stress* hardly affects us. Of course, we know the effects of stress never fade, but often, the punch of the word itself does. Still, I'm facing stress today; help me deal with it appropriately. Let me not take it out on my family or dump it on my coworkers. Help me remember to take it to You and leave it there in exchange for Your peace and strength. Amen.

Praise be to the Lord, to God our Savior, who daily bears our burdens.
PSALM 68:19 NIV

Never Really Alone

Heavenly Father, I'm lonely today. There is no one with whom I can share what is going on in my life right now. Oh, I have friends, but no one who would really understand this. But You created me, and You know me like no one else. I ask You today to let me feel Your presence with me. It's a terrible thing to be alone, but You promised You'd never leave. So, I know You are with me. I'm grateful for Your constant love and care. In Jesus' name, amen.

God has said: "I will never leave you nor forsake you."
HEBREWS 13:5 PHILLIPS

More Blessed to Give

Jesus, You are the ultimate giver. You gave up Your life on the cross. Help me give on a daily basis, not just on special occasions. Give me eyes to see people in need, whether they are in need of material blessings or simply my time. Make me a generous giver of all that You have entrusted to me. May my resources and talents flow freely rather than stagnating as I hoard them. Amen.

I have shewed you all things, how that so labouring ye ought to support the weak, and to remember the words of the Lord Jesus, how he said, It is more blessed to give than to receive.
ACTS 20:35

A Cheerful Giver

*I*t is a privilege to give to Your kingdom, heavenly Father. Whether I am writing out my tithe check or giving of my time and talents on a mission trip, let me give with joy. I have learned that You provide. I cannot "out-give" my God! You are too loving, too generous, too great! Regardless of my circumstances, mold my heart that I might always give with cheerfulness. Amen.

Every man according as he purposeth in his heart, so let him give;
not grudgingly, or of necessity: for God loveth a cheerful giver.
2 Corinthians 9:7

Tithing

*F*ather, You tell me to test You with my tithe. If I give it generously, You will bless my household. I will find it overflowing with blessings. There will not be enough room to contain all of it. I imagine the windows of heaven opening and blessings just pouring, pouring, pouring down on me! You are not a God who sprinkles blessings or gives them in little pinches or samples. You are an extravagant giver. Amen.

Bring ye all the tithes into the storehouse, that there may be meat in mine house, and prove me now herewith, saith the LORD of hosts, if I will not open you the windows of heaven, and pour you out a blessing, that there shall not be room enough to receive it.

MALACHI 3:10

Where Is My Treasure?

God, You have blessed me with good things. I treasure my family and friends. I find happiness in decorating my home and hosting parties. My job is a big part of my identity. I enjoy shopping and putting together a new outfit. It feels good to get a compliment occasionally! But where is my treasure? If these things begin to take priority over You, I know that my heart is in the wrong place. Amen.

For where your treasure is, there will your heart be also.
MATTHEW 6:21

Waiting on God

*M*y feet are positioned at the starting line. I'm ready to run the race. All I need now is Your signal for me to begin it. I believe I've found my passion, and I'm ready to act on it, but I know I need to wait for Your timing. Help me be patient. Alert me to what I still need to do in making my preparations.

I long, yes, I faint with longing to enter the courts of the LORD.
With my whole being, body and soul, I will shout joyfully to the living God.
PSALM 84:2 NLT

Calm amid the Storm

Lord, I'm running late today! Before I even got out of bed, the day seemed to go haywire! I overslept, had to skip breakfast, had a horrible commute, forgot to thaw the entrée for tonight's dinner, *and* had a few tense words with my family. So I feel really out of sorts and have this premonition that I'm going to be playing catch-up all day long. Help me focus on You on this ill-fitting day and let my attitude not match it! Amen.

"You will keep him in perfect peace, whose mind is stayed on You."
ISAIAH 26:3 NKJV

Never Too Far for You

*M*oving is highly overrated, God. Oh how I hate the disarray of boxes and the jumbled schedule involved! Moving means so many details to oversee—address change, new bank accounts, a new driver's license, new doctors and dentists, new stores, new driving routine, and on and on. Help me, Lord, adjust as smoothly as possible. And thank You that no matter where I unpack my boxes, You're already there. Amen.

"If I rise on the wings of the dawn, if I settle on the far side of the sea, even there your hand will guide me, your right hand will hold me fast."
Psalm 139:9–10 niv

Rest for a While

*I*t's vacation time, God, and am I ever ready! There's nothing like a few days of relaxation! I'm glad You built the concept of rest into the structure of our world. On the seventh day of creation, You rested. And You even designed laws for the Old Testament Hebrews so they would *have* to rest. (You knew those workaholics would ignore the Sabbath if the consequences weren't serious!) And now, I have the chance to take some time off for rest. Because of You, I am going to enjoy it to the fullest! Amen.

"Now come along to some quiet place by yourselves, and rest for a little while."
MARK 6:31 PHILLIPS

Choose Life

*J*esus, You offered me life, not just life after death but eternal life that started the day I asked You to live in my heart. Help me remember that every choice I make is a choice for life or for death, for blessing or cursing. I don't want to live one day less on the earth because of a poor choice I made. Help me make every decision count.

Today I ask heaven and earth to be witnesses. I am offering you life or death, blessings or curses. Now, choose life! Then you and your children may live.
DEUTERONOMY 30:19 NCV

Shared Comfort

*M*y friend lost a family member this week, God. I don't know what to say. I've been trying to work out the right words, but every one of them seems superficial and unfeeling to my ears. I don't want to be insensitive, but neither do I want to be melodramatic. Please, Father, guide my words; speak comfort through my lips today. Like those who have come alongside me in my dark hours, let me minister to my hurting friend today. Amen.

For he gives us comfort in our trials so that we in turn may be able to give the same sort of strong sympathy to others in theirs.

2 Corinthians 1:4 Phillips

Homeless

*F*ather, today I was approached by a homeless person and, mentally, I recoiled. I admit that I struggle with uncertainty in this kind of situation. I've heard stories about supposedly homeless people who either just don't want to work or are too incapacitated to hold down a job. Yet I'm conflicted when I recall Your words that when we care for those who are naked, cold, and hungry, we are actually serving You. Give me discernment, Lord. I can't minister in every type of environment, but if there is someone I need to touch, please prompt me. In Jesus' name, amen.

"I was hungry and you gave Me food; I was thirsty and you gave Me drink; I was a stranger and you took Me in."
MATTHEW 25:35 NKJV

Considering Flowers

Creator God, I am always amazed by the things You've made. The flowers blooming outside this summer are so delicate, yet so durable. From tiny seeds or bulbs they push forth toward the sun, breaking through the soil and raising up in fragile beauty. Petals soft as velvet and deep in color, the flowers add grace to the countryside. Yet they are incredibly strong. With the sun and rain You provide, they remain all season, delighting our eyes and hearts. Thank You for blessing us with their beauty and using them as a reminder that we need not worry. Amen.

And why take ye thought for raiment? Consider the lilies of the field.
MATTHEW 6:28

The Sea

*F*ather, I stand beside the ocean and gaze in wonder once again. What a vast expanse it is! The Bible tells us You formed the seas on the third day of Creation. It must have been an incredible sight—the waters being gathered together. And the seashore is one of my favorite places. I love to walk along the beach, scooping damp sand with my toes, hearing the cry of the gulls, and tasting the salty breeze. Thank You, Lord, for sharing Your sea with me. I feel close to You in this vastness. Amen.

The sea is his, and he made it.
Psalm 95:5

Common Sparrows

Out there on the grass, searching for food on this winter day, are common sparrows. This scene reminds me of a scripture verse in which You say that, although You do care about one little sparrow, You care much more about me. And that I should never be afraid, for I am worth much more to You than many sparrows. I revel in the fact that I am precious in Your sight! I don't have to strive for Your attention, for I am important in Your eyes! Thank You for reminding me today that I'm valued and loved. Amen.

"Not a single sparrow falls to the ground without your Father's knowledge. . . . Never be afraid, then—you are far more valuable than sparrows."
MATTHEW 10:29, 31 PHILLIPS

What's Ahead

*F*ather God, sometimes I wish I could see the future, but other times I'm glad I cannot. I doubt that knowing what is going to happen, and when, would make life any easier. So, teach me to focus on today, on this moment. Help me put my worries and anxieties in Your hands and leave the future to the One who determines it. In Christ's name, amen.

"It is not for you to know times or seasons which the Father has put in His own authority.
ACTS 1:7 NKJV

Memories

Thank You, heavenly Father, for giving me the ability to recall happy times from the past. No one can ever take those memories away from me. The moments and emotions stored in my mind can't be dumped into the "recycle bin" or erased from the disc by someone else. Memories define us and sometimes give us the inspiration to continue on. I'm grateful to have so many happy ones. Amen.

"Let them show the former things, what they were, that we may consider them, and know the latter end of them."

ISAIAH 41:22 NKJV

Messengers and Warriors

*D*ear Lord, thank You for angels—Your messengers and warriors. The stories of those who've encountered these heavenly beings fascinate me. I wonder if I've ever met an angel and didn't know it? You have a vast host of angels at Your command and often dispatch them for our good. Yet, on the cross, You did not call them to Your own aid. Instead, You willingly gave Your life for me, and now the angels want to understand that kind of love. How awesome is Your amazing love for a woman like me. Amen.

Even angels long to look into these things.
1 Peter 1:12 niv

Sensory Joys

*D*ear God, thank You for the five senses—sight, sound, touch, smell, and taste. You could have designed a virtual world, but instead You created one that can be experienced. Today I want to revel in the fact that I'm alive. I want to delight in the tactile joys I often take for granted. I'm grateful for each one. Amen.

For in him we live, and move, and have our being.
Acts 17:28

Animal Friends

Thank You for creating the animals in our world. Though they aren't on the same value scale as humans, they are a wonderful testament to Your love for living things, and they bring glory to You just by being what they are. Help me always be kind to the animals You have given us. May I be a good caretaker of Your property. Thank You for not only pets, but the wild creatures as well. Amen.

"For You created all things, and by Your will they exist and were created."
REVELATION 4:11 NKJV

Trust in His Guidance

*F*ather, this morning I come before You and I praise You. You are good and loving. You have only my very best interest at heart. Take my hand and lead me. Show me the way to go. Like a child being carried in a loving parent's arms, let me relax and trust You. I know that You will never lead me astray. Thank You, God, for this assurance. Amen.

Cause me to hear thy lovingkindness in the morning; for in thee do I trust: cause me to know the way wherein I should walk; for I lift up my soul unto thee.

PSALM 143:8

....

....

....

....

....

....

....

....

....

....

....

....

....

....

....

....

....

A Testimony

*M*y life is a song of praise to You, my faithful Father, the giver of life! When people hear my testimony of Your goodness, may they come to know You. I want others to notice the difference in me and wonder why I have such joy, such peace. May I point them to You, Lord, and may they trust in You for salvation. You are the way, the truth, and the life. Amen.

And he hath put a new song in my mouth, even praise unto our God: many shall see it, and fear, and shall trust in the LORD.
PSALM 40:3

....

....

....

....

....

....

....

....

....

....

....

....

A Thankful Heart

Lord, everything good in my life comes from You. Often I forget to say thank You. I am thankful for Your provision and Your protection. I am thankful for my family and friends. I am most of all thankful for the joy of my salvation, which comes through Christ. Give me a grateful heart, I pray. Let me always remember that every good and perfect gift comes from Your hand. Amen.

And let the peace of God rule in your hearts, to the which also
ye are called in one body; and be ye thankful.
COLOSSIANS 3:15

Love Is of God

*G*od, how will others know that I am a Christian? They will know it by my love. As I go through this day, give me opportunities to express love. It may be through a kind word of encouragement, an act of kindness, or even just a smile. Put the people in my path and on my heart today that need to experience Your love through me. Use me as a vessel of Your love. Amen.

Beloved, let us love one another: for love is of God; and every one that loveth is born of God, and knoweth God.

1 John 4:7

Loving My Neighbors

*J*esus, You did not stop with the first commandment. The second is strong as well. You tell me to love my neighbor. But You don't stop there. You tell me to love my neighbor as myself. But my neighbors are not always easy to love! Still, this is Your command. You have given me Your Holy Spirit. May I love with Your Spirit, for my own is lacking. Amen.

And the second is like, namely this, Thou shalt love thy neighbour as thyself.
There is none other commandment greater than these.
MARK 12:31

Love Covers Sins

Lord, all of my sin was nailed to the cross when Your Son died for me. Without grace, I am but filthy rags before a holy God. But through Christ, I am adopted as Your daughter, forgiven. There is pride in this daughter, God. Pride that resists forgiveness. Pride that says "I am right." Remind me of the multitude of my own sins that Your love covered through Jesus. Help me love others well. Amen.

Hatred stirreth up strifes: but love covereth all sins.
PROVERBS 10:12

The Hope of Heaven

*G*od, I cannot even imagine heaven. But I know it will be a glorious place. I know that there will be no more tears there. You tell me that in Your Word. Even the sweetest worship of my God that I take part in on this earth is nothing like the worship there. Constantly we will worship You, Father! You have prepared a place for me there. What hope I have in You. Amen.

In my Father's house are many mansions: if it were not so, I would have told you.
I go to prepare a place for you.
JOHN 14:2

The Return of Jesus Christ

*J*esus, I know that You will return. I find great hope in the scriptures that give a preview of that day! We don't know everything about it. We certainly cannot predict the timing of it. But the Bible assures us that You are coming back! This world is temporal. It shall all pass away one day. I am so thankful that I know beyond a shadow of a doubt that my Savior is coming back. Amen.

And then shall they see the Son of man coming in the clouds with great power and glory. And then shall he send his angels, and shall gather together his elect from the four winds, from the uttermost part of the earth to the uttermost part of heaven.

MARK 13:26–27

Today!

*F*ather in heaven, I have a tendency to try to live a week or month at a time. It's difficult for me to limit myself to one day, one hour, one minute. But that's how You want me to live. You know that projecting into the future causes me to wonder and worry about things that haven't happened yet. You also know that I can't be any good to anyone if my head is in the clouds, thinking about the future. So help me live in today—it's all I have at the moment. Amen.

"Does He not see my ways, and count all my steps?"
JOB 31:4 NKJV

New Compassions

I really didn't want to get up this morning, Father. My blankets seemed like good protection from the cares of the day. But when I saw the glorious sunrise and heard the cheerful, singing birds, I was reminded that Your compassions are new every morning. I knew everything would be fine. Thank You for Your faithfulness.

Sing unto the LORD, bless his name; shew forth his salvation from day to day.
PSALM 96:2

Letting Go of Bitterness

Bitterness is like cancer, God. It grows and takes over, squeezing out life. I don't want to be marked or consumed by bitterness. Let me not hold to the injustices I've experienced. Help me accept Your healing touch and let go of the beginnings of bitterness in my soul. As Joseph noted in the Old Testament, You can turn things meant for evil into good. Please do that in my life. In Christ's name, amen.

Pursue peace with all people, and holiness, without which no one will see the Lord.
HEBREWS 12:14 NKJV

When I'm Not Prepared

*F*ather God, I've put myself in a bind because I procrastinated. I knew this was looming ahead of me, but I wanted to do other things first. Or, at least, I wanted to leave the task until the right time. But now, there is no more time, and I'm not prepared. Please help me, Lord, working all things to my good. Amen.

Make the most of every opportunity.
EPHESIANS 5:16 NLT

He's in Control

Thank You, Lord, that You have a perfect plan for my life. I know I don't always understand it, but You know what's best, and everything that happens is for a reason—that You might be glorified. I'm so glad that You are in control and that I need not worry. Amen.

The LORD recompense thy work, and a full reward be given thee of the LORD God of Israel, under whose wings thou art come to trust.

RUTH 2:12

Good Judgment

Lord, I am determined to discount my own wisdom and acknowledge You in all I do. Give me a heart that discerns Your ways from my own and those of the world. Help me be sensible and practical—I don't want to over-think a situation, but I want to respond to Your direction. Help me recognize wisdom as the most valuable thing I could attain.

If you live wisely, you will live a long time; wisdom will add years to your life.
PROVERBS 9:11 NCV

Love in Deed and Truth

Father, it is easy to say the words "I love you," but it is harder to live them. You want Your children to love their enemies. You tell us to love through action and with truth. These are high callings that require Your Holy Spirit working in us. Use me as a vessel of love today in my little corner of the world. Let me love through my deeds and not just with words. Amen.

My little children, let us not love in word, neither in tongue; but in deed and in truth.
1 JOHN 3:18

Bless His Name

*J*esus, You alone are worthy of all of my praise. I bless Your name. One day I will worship You with no end, no holding back, and no earthly distraction. I will worship You in heaven forever and ever. . .with the angels and with all of Your people. For today I go into Your world, and I will choose to bless Your name in the present. Accept my offering of praise. Amen.

And I beheld, and I heard the voice of many angels round about the throne and the beasts and the elders: and the number of them was ten thousand times ten thousand, and thousands of thousands; saying with a loud voice, Worthy is the Lamb that was slain to receive power, and riches, and wisdom, and strength, and honour, and glory, and blessing.

REVELATION 5:11–12

....
....
....
....
....
....
....
....
....
....
....
....
....

The Beauty of the Lord

May my pursuit of You, Lord, be my "one thing." May I praise You and serve You in this life, which is but a training camp for eternity! I look forward to heaven, Father, where I may truly know the depths of Your beauty. I see glimpses of Your beauty in Your creation. One day it will be fully revealed. What a glorious day that will be! Until then, be my "one thing." I love You, Lord. Amen.

One thing have I desired of the LORD, that will I seek after; that I may dwell in the house of the LORD all the days of my life, to behold the beauty of the LORD, and to inquire in his temple.

PSALM 27:4 NKJV